Green Magic

THE SACRED CONNECTION TO NATURE

The practitioner of Green Magic lives a magical life in which nothing is taken for granted. She is connected to Nature, aware and appreciative of its sacred rhythms and portents. She observes the rising and setting of the Sun, the phases of the Moon, and the movements of the planets and constellations. She pays attention to the taste of the air, the smell of the Earth, the waving wildflowers, and the behavior of birds and animals. She celebrates the changing of the seasons.

Talking to plants, letting the trees know you appreciate the beauty of their turning leaves, greeting birds and butterflies, and speaking to the clouds are part of the practice of Green Magic—you are extending your awareness into your surroundings. Do not be surprised if things you never noticed before start to catch your attention, because once you start extending your awareness, the indwelling animal and plant spirits around you will respond.

About the Author

Ann Moura (Aoumiel) has been a solitary practitioner of Green Witch-craft for over thirty-five years. She derived her Craft name, Aoumiel, to reflect her personal view of the balance of the male and female aspects of the Divine. Her mother and grandmother were Craftwise Brazilians of Celtic-Iberian descent who, while operating within a general framework of Catholicism, passed along a heritage of folk magic and Craft concepts that involved spiritism, ancient Celtic deities, herbal spells, Green magic, reincarnation belief, and rules for using "The Power."

The Craft was approached casually in her childhood, being experienced or used as situations arose. With the concepts of candle spells, herbal relationships to magic, spiritism, reincarnation, Rules of Conduct, and calling upon the Elementals and the Divine already established through her mother's teachings in particular, she was ready to proceed in her own direction with the Craft by the time she was fifteen. In her practice of the Craft today, Aoumiel has moved away from the Christianized associations used by her mother and grandmother. She is focused on the basic Green level of Witchcraft and is teaching the next generation in her family. She took both her Bachelor of Arts and Master of Arts degrees in history. She is married, has a daughter and a son, and is a certified history teacher at the high school level.

To Write to the Author

If you wish to contact the author or would like more information about this book, please write to the author in care of Llewellyn Worldwide and we will forward your request. Both the author and publisher appreciate hearing from you and learning of your enjoyment of this book. Llewellyn Worldwide cannot guarantee that every letter written to the author will be answered, but all will be forwarded. Please write to:

Ann Moura (Aoumiel)
% Llewellyn Worldwide
P.O. Box 64383, Dept. 0-7387-0181-5
St. Paul, MN 55164-0383, U.S.A.

Please include a self-addressed, stamped envelope with your letter.
If outside the U.S.A., enclose international postal coupons.

GREEN MAGIC

THE SACRED CONNECTION TO NATURE

ANN MOURA
(AOUMIEL)

2002
Llewellyn Publications
St. Paul, Minnesota 55164-0383, U.S.A.

FIRST EDITION
First Printing, 2002

Cover design by Lisa Novak
Cover photo by Lisa Novak
Editing and design by Connie Hill
Interior illustrations by Nyease Somerset

Library of Congress Cataloging-in-Publication Data
Aoumiel / Moura, Ann
    Green magic : the sacred connection to nature / Ann Moura
    (Aoumiel) — 1st ed.
      p.   cm. —
    Includes bibliographical references (p. 207) and index.
    ISBN 0–7387–0181–5 (pbk)
    1. Magic. 2. Plants—Miscellanea. I. Title.
BF1623.P5 A59   20020
133.4'3—dc21   2001050671

Llewellyn Publications
A Division of Llewellyn Worldwide, Ltd.
P.O. Box 64383, Dept. 0–7387–0181–5
St. Paul, Minnesota 55164-0383, U.S.A.
http://www.llewellyn.com

 Printed in the United States of America on recycled paper

Dedication

With *Perfect Love and Perfect Trust* put into practice, through the Elementals and the Divine, this book is dedicated to all Seekers, magic workers, and energy movers. Take from these pages what you need to work your personal magic, and live in union and awareness of your connection with one another.

Other Books by Ann Moura

Dancing Shadows: The Roots of Western Religious Beliefs
  (as Aoumiel)

Green Witchcraft: Folk Magic, Fairy Lore & Herb Craft

Green Witchcraft II: Balancing Light and Shadow

Origins of Modern Witchcraft

Green Witchcraft III: The Manual

Contents

Acknowledgements

I want to thank the people who have continued to encourage me to write about my family Craft. From my husband and my children to the readers and the many individuals at Llewellyn who help put together the book you hold in your hands, without any one of them this would not be possible. There is a feeling of family and community among those who contribute to this effort, no matter what the background, and this is what makes the publication of a book all the more exciting and meaningful. I especially thank Nancy Mostad for her unwavering support, Connie Hill for her clear-sighted perspective on the editing process, the artists and layout people for their care and skill in design, Natalie Harter for working closely with me in the publicity department—Goddess knows that is no easy task—and to those wonderful people who have the courage to take another writer's manuscript, read it, make their remarks and wait for the ice shards to fly. It takes a lot of cooperation between a lot of people; it takes respect for each person providing input into a manuscript project; and it takes a lot of love and hard work to make it all come together in a book that sits patiently on the shelf awaiting the opportunity to offer its contents to the willing reader. Here in your hands, then, lies the labor of many more people than just the author. Feel the texture of the pages, embrace the designs, and most of all, enjoy the magic!

SPELL CREATING
AND CASTING

Introduction

The Craft, Wicca, Witchcraft, and the Old Religion are all names for the spirituality that holds a holistic view of the world in which each of us is related to all life through the flow of universal energy. How that energy is gathered, directed, and worked with forms the basis of magical practice in Witchcraft, for magic is the art of creating changes according to your will. To successfully practice magic, you must understand that the energy flow is real, and that it is Divine.

This book is focused on the mechanics of energy raising and manipulation—how the magic works and how to put your Craft elements together for successful spell work. Because this book is about the components of magic in the Green Craft, there will necessarily be some information here that has been touched upon in one of my previous three books about my family tradition: *Green Witchcraft: Folk Magic, Fairy Lore, & Herb Craft* (Llewellyn 1996) provides some background for

1

Green spell crafting; *Green Witchcraft II: Balancing Light & Shadow* (Llewellyn 1999) identifies tools and correspondences that relate to the Dark Aspects of the Divine; and *Green Witchcraft III: The Manual* (Llewellyn 2000) presents the course I occasionally teach. Between these three books, a student has at hand sufficient material to construct spells and perform ritual magic, but here I want to delve into the components of what Green magic is and what the practitioner is capable of doing with it. Unlike the other books, however, this book contains no Esbat and Sabbat information, no Rites of Passage, no spells, no guided meditations, and no divination material. Whenever appropriate, I will refer the reader to sections in these other books for further reading. Additionally, I feel that while there are some concepts and bits of information here that may be gleaned from the other three books, not everyone who reads this book will have read the others, and so these are relevant to creating a complete picture in one place on the practice of magic. The many lists of correspondences so vital to the crafting of spells are collated from the other three and placed in Appendix A of this book. The intent of this particular book is to examine how the magic works, utilizing the methods and psychology behind the Green Craft as I learned them, so a person will be able to enhance their own magical practice.

Wicca today is basically a modern revival of the pre-Judeo-Christian view of the universe, and sees our place within it as intrinsic partners with Nature rather than standing apart from Nature. The Green Craft that I write about is what I learned from my mother, and she from her mother. While I have no documentation or first-hand knowledge of Craft practices prior to the 1890 beginnings of my maternal grandmother, it seems reasonable to me that since her maternal line is Iberian Celt (from Galicia), the family tradition has most likely bubbled along quietly for some time. I grew up with Nature magics and Elemental connections; candle magics and spell crafting; Rules of Conduct and spiritism; meditations and positive visualizations; all of which I still practice today, and which I have passed along to my now-adult children. We never added the "k" to the end of the word "magic(k)" as is often done in Craft writings to distinguish it from stage magic, tricks, or sleight-of-hand, but this additional letter is a growing trend in Craft writing. To me, the context of Witchcraft, especially among practitioners, makes the meaning of the word self-evident, so I will continue with the spelling to which I am accustomed, with only the statement that this book does not discuss stage magic, tricks, or sleight-of-hand. The Green Craft, then, is very natural, practical, grounded, and Earth centered. Before launching into the nuts and bolts of Craft magic, however, a brief review of Green Witchcraft is in order.

Green Witchcraft is the Old Religion, grounded in the powers of Nature, formed in a time when people interacted as communal, social equals, addressing the Goddess and the God as the powerful forces of Nature. The term "Green" describes the prevalence of herbal use, the approach of Witchcraft through Nature and the Elementals, and the imagery of the Divine as the Lord and Lady of the Greenwood, or the Wildwood—as Mother Earth and Horned God—emblems of fertility, power, and all-encompassing love. In many ancient Western societies, the color green is also associated with Fairie, the Other People, and those Nature-attuned people who commune with them. The Green level Craft is the foundation of all magic tradition, harkening to a time before the development of social stratas requiring deities to represent and authorize the assumed power of rulers, law makers, the supporting priesthood, and warrior class who enforced the new system. Instead, the Green Craft retains the natural magical relationship with the energies of the Earth from which a variety of Pagan and Witchcraft Traditions have arisen.

The Green Witch is a Natural Witch, a Hereditary Witch, a Kitchen Witch, a Cottage Witch, a Hedge Witch (a rustic itinerant Witch who pauses along the roadside hedgerows to create charms and other spells for people), and generally, a Solitary Witch (one who works alone or only within a small family group). The Green Witch does not fear Nature and the woods, but finds both comforting and homey, having a sense of belonging and connection with the Earth and the universe. The practice of the Green Craft draws the powers of Nature into the individual to create changes through magical workings. This power is not intangible or amorphous, but palpable energy that can be brought into your own energy field to work in conjunction with your energies and through you to achieve your goals without draining yourself.

With the arrival of social-hierarchy religions, the power of Divine Nature was denied to the people, with the rituals then confined to an elite priesthood while the rest of society participated peripherally as observers or in less important associated activities. But the old ways persisted, often hidden among the people and passed along through generations as folk magics, superstitions, and even as practices incorporated with one pretext or another into the new religions. In this way, the sacred days of Paganism, most notably Ostara, Yule, and Samhain, became the holidays of modern religions, complete with the earlier Pagan customs of bunnies, eggs, and baskets; decorated tree, presents, and an elder gift-giver (Saturn, the Holly King, and now Santa Claus); and All Souls' Eve Mass (Roman Catholic) with candlelight church services at midnight. Other Pagan holy days, including Lughnassadh and Imbolc, became *saint's days*, incorporating Pagan customs. Returning to the Nature foundation of the Green Practice awakens the ancient spirituality of our ancestors within us, however, and because of this, many people who turn to the Wiccan path say they feel that they are "coming home." This is to be expected, actually, because they are in fact returning to their spiritual roots.

There are three basic approaches to the Green Craft available to the practitioner. The Craft may be considered folk magics under a mainstream religion, often with the religious figures of the social religion viewed in Pagan terms—Saint Francis as the Greenman, for example, or Mary as the Goddess and Jesus as the God. There are images that may be drawn from other religious backgrounds as well. The angels, archangels, saints, prophets, apostles, and so forth all have attributes that may be utilized in focusing the power. Ceremonial Magicians use a Judaic-Christian framework in their practices, and many Eastern deities that are currently reverenced have been adopted by modern Pagans.

Witchcraft may also be practiced by working directly with the energies of Nature without reference to deities, ignoring the trappings of religion altogether, in which case a work area rather than an altar is used. This kind of Green Craft calls upon the power drawn through uniting with Nature the Mannuz (my mother pronounced this *Mahn-nu*—The Self—related perhaps to the Runic symbol Mannaz). Success comes from working *for* your Self rather than *against* another's Self, and this style of practice is very energizing on a personal level.

The third method is that of religion, working through and with the Divine as the Lady and the Lord, the Goddess and the God. If you want to practice the Craft while remaining within the socially accepted fold of mainstream religion, the first style is for you. If you want to work without religious connotations, simply to be connected with Nature, the second style is for you. If you seek spiritual fulfillment through connection with the Divine along with oneness with Nature, then the third style may suit your needs. I have utilized all three approaches successfully, so I know all three work. It is simply a matter of what is comfortable for you in the current stage of your life.

To work with the Deities, you may want to attune yourself to aspects with which you are familiar, or that you feel drawn to. Yet, I feel that choosing names for the Divine in the Green Craft is not especially important, simply because most of the deity names we know are merely titles or descriptions of Divine aspects turned into proper nouns in another or archaic language. In the Northern Tradition, as an example, the God and the Goddess of Nature are Frey and Freya—names that translate as *Lord* and *Lady*—while in other cultures there are deity names translating as *Beneficent, Good Goddess, Abundance, Bear Lady,* and *Star Lady.* For the working of magic, it is sufficient to know in your own mind what influence is being sought rather than what name matches that influence; thus I feel that a generic "Lady and Lord" can prove more effective because this does not confine the deity to a limited aspect.

While you may research various pantheons (Greek, Roman, Etruscan, Celtic, Northern European, Mesopotamian, Minoan, Egyptian, Indian, Oriental, Polynesian, Native American, and so forth) and learn the myths of the various Gods and Goddesses in order to select an appropriate patron and patroness deity, you may also have a successful practice using various generic terms for the Divine, such as Lady/Lord; Goddess/God; Great Lady/Great Lord; Great Mother/Great Father; or the Ancient Ones. After a Dedication Ritual used to embark upon this third style of practice (ritual begins on page 152 of *Green Witchcraft; Folk Magic, Fairy Lore & Herb Craft*), when the Divine gives the practitioner a secret name to use in ritual and spell work, you may ask for their own secret names, which they will reveal for a more personal connection to them. This is a *trust*, and you must not divulge this to others, for it is your personal link to the Divine.

Many of the key issues of magical use are guided by the Witches' Rede, a lengthy rhyme created at least in part by Gerald Gardner and Doreen Valiente. The string of proverbs (reminiscent of a scene from *Hamlet* in which Polonius advises his son Laertes with proverbs, including avoiding the company of fools) is most often presented with the salient parts in one piece:

> *Bide the Witches' Rede ye must; in perfect love and perfect*
> *trust. Eight words the Rede thou must fulfill: An' it harm*
> *none, do as ye will. What ye send forth returns to thee, so*
> *ever mind the rule of three. Follow this with mind and heart,*
> *and merry ye meet and merry ye part.*

Most Witches generally accept the rule of "If it harms none, do what you will," as the key to their practice, and not all accept the idea of threefold returns. With the basic tenet of harming none being followed, everything else is a matter of selecting what actually works for you. Using this principle, the Witch determines what change is desired and how to set about achieving the desired result.

The modern Witches' Rede is very similar to the **Rules of Conduct** my mother told me her mother repeated to her as she was growing up. My mother solemnly intoned these same rules throughout my childhood and early teen years so that they became part of my life. She said:

> **Be careful what you do. Be careful who you trust. Do**
> **not use the power to hurt another, for what is sent**
> **comes back. Never use the power against someone who**

***has the power. To use the power, you must feel it in
your heart, and know it in your mind.***

These words and her tone and manner of presenting them meant
to me that magic is not a game, but a sacred act, involving a genuine
connection with the Divine: the Divine in the Elementals, the Divine
in Nature, and the Divine within each of us. We must use care in
what we do so as not to harm one another or ourselves, and we
must recognize that other Witches are our kindred. My mother
would often add after the injunction not to use the power against
someone who has the power, ***"for you both draw from the same
well."***

In modern Wicca, there is a Law of Threefold Return, which
states that what you send returns to you threefold. My mother only
spoke of what is sent returning, meaning that the energy you generate and send outward will attract like energy back to you. The
"knowing" of this energy means that it is *not* an act of faith, but of
understanding a different aspect of reality—it is *fact* that is felt and
comprehended, and so of course it works. Magic, then, is a great
responsibility, and you must take this to heart in your practice of
the Craft. In these pages I am presenting information based on my
mother's instruction and on my own developing practice.

There are variations in what I do from what is taught in many
Traditions, but this information is part of my family heritage, which
I lay before you to use as selectively as you feel appropriate. Magic is
generated through spell work of one sort or another, but in using
another's spells, always make a change, either through substitution,
alteration, deletion, or addition to make it *your* spell, to tie it and the
desired results to *you*. It is my hope that with this book, the practitioner will be able to more clearly understand the magical process
and how these rules apply, in order to more effectively select the
method and focus to direct raised magical energies successfully.

Magical Practice

There is a general impression that Witchcraft operates solely as *sympathetic magic*—the concept that all things are linked together by energy fields—but this type of magic forms only one aspect of the magical practice. With Green Witchcraft, magic is differentiated by the components involved and the usage; by the *purpose* and by the *method*. Some people speak of white, black, and even gray Witchcraft (the latter inferring something in between), but in my experience, these are terms associated with the good/evil polarization of modern religious thinking and have nothing to do with the Old Religion. Witches act in attunement with the Earth and Nature, practicing spiritually connective rites with balance, not dichotomy.

Dichotomy is a feature of modern societies (the past 2,000–3,000 years, depending on the locale—see my book, *Origins of Witchcraft: The Evolution of a World Religion,* Llewellyn, 2000), not ancient societies and cultures. With this modern view, white (or light) is associated with "good" and black (or dark and shadow) with "evil." Gray is some sort of mixture of good and evil, becoming what I like to call an ambiguous spiritual soup. None of this is part of the Craft as I was taught it by my mother and grandmother—they taught balance and interconnection.

When I was very young, my mother and my grandmother took me to a forest by a lake where we stayed in a little cabin for a few days. There, I quickly spotted an owl that had taken up residence in the roof rafters of the screened porch, and a snake that swam in the shallows next to a small rowboat when I was set in it to play by my mother and grandmother while they watched. I was fascinated by these creatures as my grandmother held me in her arms in the cool outdoors and lovingly talked to me about them. Although I was only three years old at the time, the images of the owl and snake by the cabin at the edge of the dim woods and dark lake have never left me. The time we spent there has gained special significance for me over the intervening years: for awhile, we were maiden, mother, and crone in the wilds of Nature, watched over by the emblems of the Goddess and the God. Is it any wonder that the images have been imprinted on my mind? This is how magic works—*naturally*, not forced or strained at, but gentle and pervasive. Once it is felt, you will never forget the sensations that accompany it and will recognize it in your spell work.

The rituals of Green Witchcraft may be carefully planned and conducted or they may be spontaneous and fresh. The items used in spell work are often of natural materials so as to engage the essences and powers of the life-force within. The Green Witch respects the powers and spirits of Nature, and in working with them, knows that these energies never die, but may be directed to accomplish a goal. Thus, when using an herb for a purpose in a spell, the energy of that herb is addressed and called upon to work with you in creating the effect you desire. When you burn the herb in a candle during a ritual, you are releasing that energy to blend with your own for directing it in your magics. That energy, once focused on a goal, is then sent to work the magic—to create the desired changes.

With most magics, the objects of Nature—stones, water, herbs, trees, plants, shells, clay, soil, feathers, creatures, and even clouds and the air (seen as the Four Winds)—take on special significance. These are all kinfolk to us, related through the life energy of the God expressed through the manifesting forms of the Goddess. Because we are interrelated, we must respect our kin in Nature, of which we are a part, and ask these objects for their help in our work, never taking from Nature without permission.

The Green Practice utilizes herbs in spellwork, magical teas, healing, and folkcrafts, and by using the objects in Nature, the Green Witch is able to construct spells with materials that are readily at hand. These spells, charms, and other magics work through the Elementals, the four basic powers of Witchcraft and magical practice: Earth, Air, Fire, and Water. My previous books have provided tables of correspondences for a useable Spellbook, or Book of Shadows, and in *Green Witchcraft III*, I suggested pages for tabbing in *Green Witchcraft* to make the book a more useable tool in your practice and for use as a text for the course of study. With Green-level magics, there are associations made to herbs and other plants, impressions that colors create on the spirit and mind, and energies evoked in nonherbal items of Nature such as feathers, rocks, sticks, pebbles, crystals, minerals, natural clay, volcanic lava, pumice, and the waters of springs, rivers, sea, and storms. The Elemental forms of Air, Water, Fire, and Earth figure in all these associations, affording a grounding in the Lady and the Lord of Nature.

The Elementals are usually addressed in Green practice, but the use of ritual in conscious spell work develops according to the preferences of the practitioner. Magical tools such as knives (a black-handled ritual knife called an athame, and a white- or brown-handled working knife called a bolline), wands, crystal balls, and divination cards will become imbued with the power of the individual Witch, so that, over time, the tools for specific intentions will be intuitively recognized. You may want to use an oak wand for some magics, a willow, elder, or hazel wand for others, and one topped with a crystal for yet another type—by using them, you develop a feel for them. Anything that you personally sense as meaningful to your objective becomes an acceptable tool for your magical use.

The understanding of the Elementals and such things as the pentagram (five-pointed star in a circle), sigils of planets, and focal words formed through a numerological planetary square (see Migene González-Wippler's *The Complete Book of Spells, Ceremonies, and Magic*, Llewellyn, 1988) or alphabetical Witch's Circle (page 57, *Green Witchcraft III*), Square, or Rectangle, will vary with each person. Some practitioners may routinely burn inscribed candles, while others prefer to tie knots in a string of yarn or burn a paper with keywords for magical action. This happens because we are all unique—no matter how similar in background, temperament, training or character, each person is an individual, whose perception of the world is Self-integrated. I like to compare people to snowflakes, because like these, no two of us are alike. Nature has an amazing capacity for vast diversity, and in this we see the living evidence of the Infinite, the Immanent Divine. Your unique perspective gives you the power to mold the natural items of the Craft and attune these to your own personal inner energies for directing.

In working magic, you will find that categorizing the properties and attributes of colors, herbs, oils, and incenses in your Spellbook or Book of Shadows (BOS) will develop this tool into a practical guide for your Craft work. The key to Witchcraft and successful magic work is being able to combine all of these elements in the formulation of your spells. But beyond mere mixing and blending (rather like the tarot card, Temperance), you have to understand what it is that you are doing. I shall therefore identify in this book the components of spells, describe the various types of spells, discuss the twin aspects of magic (purpose and method), and describe magical techniques incorporating the above so that you are able to select the best magical route for success.

Basic Components of
Spell Creating and Casting

When conducting magic in Green Witchcraft, it is through the four Elementals that you draw and focus energy. Spells are the vehicles of magical workings, thus any ritual, brew, charm, chant, prayer, amulet, talisman, or crafted item created for magical purpose, utilizing the movement of energy, the speaking of a word or formula of power, in the generating of intent into manifestation is a variety of spell crafting. Even so, the varieties of spells are usually separate terms, and the word "spell" is often used to designate a procedure. In nearly every spell, be it ritual, charm, or craft, there will be references to Earth, Air, Fire, and Water. In the Green Craft, there is a strong inclusion of *Elementalism,* but as "kinship" rather than as the dictionary description of "worship." In a ritual format, you will normally find that salt is used to represent Earth, incense smoke will convey the impression of Air, a candle flame will indicate Fire, and a bowl of *charged* water (ritually blessed and energized, thus, "holy") will symbolize Water. These images are used for blessing, consecrating, and charging other objects with the Elemental energies.

Magic is often initiated with the casting of a circle that becomes the sacred space wherein magical work is to be conducted (see Appendix B for a Basic Circle Casting Ritual). This circle acts as a barrier between the practitioner working *between the worlds* (at a gateway between planes of existence) and the outside (physical or mundane) world. It is also an energy field that concentrates and enhances the energies raised within by the practitioner.

When the magical circle is drawn, the Elementals are called upon at the Quarters to hold the circle firm and to lend their power to the work at hand, with one Elemental assigned to North, East, South, and West. In some Traditions, there are variations in which direction an Elemental is invoked and even a changing of location according to the time of day (Draconian Tradition), but for most Witchcraft the general practice places Earth at the North, Air at the East, Fire at the South, and Water at the West. The placement of the altar or work area within the circle also differs with Traditions or with the visualization needs of a particular spell, but the Green Craft usually places the altar at the North, the realm of Earth (where desires are manifested) and the seat of Wisdom (realm of the Crone), although it may be placed at the West for calling upon the Sidhe and Shadow work.

In a ritual context, certain tools are also seen as aligned with particular Elementals. With the Green Craft, the athame is considered an Air tool, being used to cast and open the ritual Circle, to raise and direct energy, and to inscribe candles (some practitioners use the bolline for this) with symbols which provide a mental or inspirational association that applies to the work being done. The wand is recognized as a Fire tool, for invoking or calling upon the Elementals, spirits, beings, and essences within a magical context. It is also used, like the athame, to raise and direct energy. In some traditions, the alignment of Fire and Air is reversed so that the athame becomes the symbol for Fire, and the wand becomes the symbol for Air. The chalice or cup represents Water, and holds a ritual beverage. The cauldron may be considered an emblem of Water, or of Spirit, since it may be used to hold the libation (offering) to the Divine (a bit of the beverage from the cup), or the workings of the spell—for it is within the cauldron of transformation that a spell may effect the magic. The pentacle represents Earth, and is a circular flat disk inscribed or engraved with a pentagram upon it—this is where spell material is combined and placed for manifestation, so you may be setting the cauldron on top of the pentacle during your spell casting. This object is often made of wood, tile, metal, stone, or ceramic, but other materials may be used so that even a pentagram drawn on paper will serve as a pentacle.

With the word choice of pentacle or pentagram, some individuals consider all jewelry or other use of the circled star as a pentagram, while others see these as a pentacle. In my experience, the word pentagram refers to a *figure*, while the word pentacle describes a five-pointed star *object*, hence, once the figure is turned into an object, I feel it has been translated from a pentagram figure (such as drawn after a signature or written spell) into a pentacle. Rings, pendants, and the ritual object on the altar may all be pentacles, while the use of the word pentagram relates only to the image of the encircled star. You might have a pentagram in the lines of your palm, for example (often associated with Werewolves, so watch out for Full Moons!), but not a pentacle. Jewelry may be considered either depending upon the presentation as the isolated object (a pentacle) or as an inscription on a background of other material such as metal or stone (a pentagram). This is how I define the use of these words.

In the working of spells, various aspects of the process are performed with an envisionment of the actions being in sets of three's. Three is a sacred number in many religious practices, but was especially so to the Celts (thus Saint Patrick used the clover as a means of associating the Celts' mystic three, the *Triskele* (TRIS-kel), or *Triskelion* (Tris-KEL-ee-on), with the Christian Trinity). Three times three, or nine, is another sacred number, being related to the Goddess and to the binding of energy to a goal. In using a ritual Circle, you could invoke the power of the number three by casting, asperging, and fuming (not raging, but spreading incense smoke around the circle—also called censing), or the power of the number nine by deliberately focusing on performing nine pacings of the Circle:

1. The area is swept

2. The area is delineated in the casting

3. The area is asperged

4. The area is censed

5. The Quarters are prepared with a candle lit or raised at each position invoking light and the quality of the Elemental at that place

6. The Elementals themselves are invoked [ritual is then conducted]

7. The Elementals are farewelled

8. The candles are extinguished at the Quarters

9. The Circle is opened

Through envisioning steps as a numerical form, the entire magical event is given the energy influence of the selected number, which in the above example is nine. If the candles at the Quarters are extinguished at the time the Elementals are farewelled, or if they are not used at the Quarters, then the power of the number nine can be fulfilled through taking the spell work itself to each Quarter and addressing the Elemental for assistance in relation to that Elemental, such as calling upon Earth to bring the spell into manifestation, Air to give the spell swift passage, Fire to energize the spell, and Water to move the spell to a satisfactory conclusion. You have to consider how each Elemental figures into the actual spell process to make this effective. Another format that utilizes the energy and binding power of the number nine is to repeat the spell wording nine times (if short enough) or to state after one casting of the words that the spell is "empowered by three times three."

Gestures are also part of the spell-working process. Your hands become tools for beseeching and invoking. Hands form gestures of blessing and unification, but they are also used to draw energy inward and to extend your own inner energies outward to others for sharing. Energy is readily released or absorbed through the palms, thus the practice of "laying on of hands" for healings. Rubbing the palms and then using your open hands to "smooth" out static energy in an aura, keeping your palms about an inch away from the person's body, is one type of healing. The negative energies are either motioned down and into the ground, or drawn into your hands from the aura being cleansed, then shaken out and released into the ground by touching the Earth with your palms. In magical practice, the hands may also be used to gather the energies of the forces called upon to be directed into the spell materials. In the exchange of energy, it is important not to deplete your own reserves, lest you become ill, tense, or nervous. This is why the practitioner should always *ground and center* (drain off your own excess or static energies, thus stilling yourself to draw up the energy of the Earth and bring it into your personal internal alignment for calm directing) before conducting any spell work, ritual, or meditation.

Grounding and centering work together to join the practitioner with the energy of the Earth, but even among Witches, the perceived order sometimes differs. I see this process as a grounding of my own excess energies, be they stress or excitement, so that I am calm, while in the same sweep I am drawing inward the powerful energy of the Earth to my inner core to be merged in solid strength and connection. No matter how you differentiate the process, what is happening is a stilling of your emotional and mental self, finding your center of quiet and energy. Some people like to focus on the *chakras* (energy points in the body), seeing the internal color energies of the red root (base of spine), orange sacral plexus (abdomen), yellow solar plexus (navel), green heart, blue throat, purple third eye (forehead), and white crown (top of the head) balanced and perhaps cleansed by bringing the white light of the crown down through all the chakras and back up. You then connect with the source of energy outside your body—with the Earth—by visualizing and feeling the energy of the Earth rising up into you. Grounding and centering is completed when you interweave the Earth's energy with your own. Once this is done, you may cast your Circle, perform your rituals and spells, then return the excess energy back to the Earth with gratitude and appreciation for the assistance given to you. This second *grounding* is when you touch the Earth (or floor if working indoors) with the palms of your hands to drain out the excess energy. This MUST be done after magical workings or you will be nervous, headachy, tense, hyper, or irritable for some time afterward.

When setting up your altar space or working area, there should be some degree of symmetry in the arrangement. This is conducive to the flow of energy. There is also a triangular aspect to this flow (incorporating the magic of three) in the flow of energy to you at the apex, and from you toward the broad base of the altar. The altar may be structured with the left side designated for the Goddess, the right side for the God, and the center for Both. Ritual objects may be placed on the altar according to the Elemental (and therefore Deity) association, with Earth and Water generally seen as Goddess elements, and Air and Fire generally seen as God elements. Thus you may have the water and salt on one side and the wand and the knife on the other along with the incense, unless you prefer a different symmetry. The idea behind feng shui is the proper placement of objects for the auspicious movement of energy, and with an altar, this is found in the setting of Craft items. I prefer to see water as Goddess-related since the Goddess of Nature is reverenced at holy wells and sacred springs, while salt is related to the God since the Horned God of Nature is an Earth God. I see the wand and the knife divided between the two, with the wand for Her and the knife for Him, and so they are placed on opposite sides on my altar. But the key here is that this is how the energy moves best for me. As long as you have a symmetrical envisionment, the arrangement of tools on an altar is as good as the energy flow you derive from it. Therefore, because of variations in Traditions, in your own personal associations, and in the aspects of the Lady and the Lord you are working with, the placements will vary. Another difference lies in the idea of what is *left* and what is *right*. For some practitioners, myself included, the left and the right are extensions of their own sides as they face the altar, but for others, the left and the right are reversed (a mirror image) from the perspective of the altar facing the practitioner. All that matters is that you are comfortable with the arrangement and it has meaning for you.

Spell Working

The objects used in magic should be cleansed and consecrated to that purpose. To prepare your athame, wand, cup, cauldron, pentacle, and other tools for magical work, pass each item through the Elementals, calling upon that Elemental to cleanse it of extraneous energies and charge it with the power of that Elemental (see Appendix C for a Tool Consecration Ritual). The tool is sprinkled with salt, passed through incense smoke, passed through candle flame, and sprinkled with blessed water. Inscribing the tool with magical signs and runes (or other such symbols), including your Craft (not Working) name, helps to align the energies to you and your purposes. You state the action you take to make the bonding complete:

> *In the names of the Goddess and the God,* (names), *I consecrate this* (name of item) *to be used in my practice of the Craft. I charge this by Elemental Earth* (touch the item to the pentacle or sprinkle with salt), *by Elemental Air* (pass through smoke), *by Elemental Fire* (pass through candle flame), *and by Elemental Water* (sprinkle with blessed water). *This tool is now by powers bound to aid me in my work. So Mote It Be!*

When charging crystals, also hold the crystal to the center of your brow, above and between your eyes (Third Eye—site of psychic power), and visualize the purpose you want this crystal to have. Some crystals are used for divination, some for balancing energies, and others for enhancing and transmitting specific types of energies. In candle magics in particular, you will want to smooth an appropriate oil (Appendix A) over the object so that the associated energy of that oil will further prepare the item for use in a spell.

Successful spell work is also encouraged by making use of timing and astrological information. Moon phases are the major influence for Witches, with the Waxing Moon promoting growth and new projects, the Full Moon bringing plans to fruition, offering healing and empowerment, the Waning Moon helping with spells that cleanse, release, or banish energies, and the Dark or New Moon bringing aid to meditations and divinations. Besides these, there are astrological influences that can be useful in choosing the timing of spell work. Each astrological body has certain attributes in magical practice, and there are planetary associations for each day of the week. By selecting a day under a particular planetary influence, you gain that planetary assistance in the raising and focusing of energies. Hours of each day, separated into twelve-hour segments after sunrise and twelve after sunset, also have planetary associations that can be drawn into the spell working. Even the weather may play a role if you add in the explosive power of storms, the gentle cleansing of soft rainfall, the coolness of winter, the heat of summer, or the calm energies of a placid day. Comets and meteor showers can be sources of energy flow as well, and may be invoked to give some spells an extra boost.

What you are doing in the construction of spells is making selections from your lists of correspondences, combining ingredients much as a chef creating a new culinary delight. You work with what is available, choosing substitutions as needed, and so you should always have more than one ingredient for a particular effect. Your lists include colors, herbal associations, incenses, oils, hours, days of the week, and runic or other symbols. After you review the available resources, you can draft your spell and ritual. Using the correspondences, the timing, and the goal you seek to achieve, you can now construct the words, the gestures, and magical associations you want to evoke.

Planning ahead keeps things moving in the right direction. Once you raise energy, unless you focus and direct it quickly, it will start to dissipate or wander about your circle. Then you will either have to clear the circle and start over, or expect lesser results. So know in advance what you will do, what you will say, and how you will utilize the energy raised. I find it quite annoying when energy has been successfully raised by a group, then is allowed to weaken or dissipate because the leader did not know when to release that energy to fulfill the task assigned. While some people might not notice the drifting of the energy, others certainly will, so, especially in group settings, do keep your focus and remember that you are working with something that becomes tangible and may need to be released sooner than your ritual had proscribed—do not drone on simply because you wrote a pretty speech.

You can place a spell within the context of an Esbat or draft a ritual specifically for the spell. In the case of the former, the spell work comes before the Cakes and Wine (or Simple Feast). I do not recommend doing spell work during a Sabbat as this event focuses energy on connection with the Divine during a celebration of a solar phase that marks a point in the calendar relating it to symbolic myths of the Goddess and the God. Unless the moon is in a special phase or other circumstances are present, Sabbats are holy days of observance on the Wheel of the Year, with energy devoted to invocations to the Divine directed more toward connectedness, community, and global welfare.

Spells do not require a lot of ritual, but can be conducted in a very straightforward manner. Casting the circle and moving right into the spell work is acceptable, and in a rush, even the circle need not be cast. You have to make the determination as to what you need to conduct a spell—that is what makes magic a craft, an art. and the best way to learn is through practice.

When you draft your spells and rituals, be as thorough as possible. Have all your tools and ingredients laid out, the altar arranged, the candles and incense lit, and perhaps notecards with your spell in steps. Think about the Elemental influences you want to use, and the Deity aspects you want to invoke. Do you need the assistance of the Goddess as Crone, Mother, or Maiden? The Great Goddess? The Sun God, the Horned Hunter, or the Lord of Shadows? Again, this takes us back to associations. All the portions of the spell should match and correlate, so that from start to finish, you are consistent in the energies raised and utilized.

The basic components of a spell ritual include determining the timing of the spell, outlining the ritual and preparing the tools and materials, but also preparing yourself and the work area or sacred space—the circle. By bathing with sea or mineral salt and a sachet of herbs you have selected for their affinity to the spell you are planning, you cleanse yourself of daily stress and alert your senses to a new awareness. This is the initial stage of reaching an altered state through which you are able to work with magical energies. Now is a good time to ground and center, drawing up into yourself the Earth energies you will need. You then sweep your sacred space with a besom (a broom used only for the circle and magical work):

> *As I sweep, may the besom chase away all negative and chaotic energies within this circle that it be cleansed and made ready for my work.*

Creating the circle comes next, then you invoke the Divine, perform the ritual observance, raise and direct energy, ground the residual power, take some refreshment, acknowledge the Divine, farewell the Elementals and open the circle, putting away your tools and disposing of spell materials. You may want to disperse a spell into a breeze, bury the remnants in the soil, or release the residue into flowing water. Normally you will not be re-using the candle, so after the spell is completed this will be disposed of as well. Crystals can be cleansed in cold running water and set on a bed of amethyst (most rock shops have these) or overnight in a bowl with sea salt. Other tools may be simply cleaned and passed through the symbols of the Elementals once more before storing.

Throughout the working, the energy will flow through you and through the natural ingredients. You weave together your own energy with that of the Earth, the herbs, the Elementals, and the Divine to create a magical event. When the spell is finished, you visualize it as completed, not as in process unless you plan to repeat the spell periodically, as when you draw something to you over a period of several days. Here is where your skill in visualizing is needed. If you cannot see the effect of the spell in your mind, then you need to practice more on visualizing.

There are a number of good visualization exercises, including imagining every detail, aroma, texture, sound, and sensation of peeling and eating a fruit (such as an orange or apple), walking in a wood, swimming in the ocean, riding a bicycle, or driving a car. To practice, select an exercise, then imagine the process step by step. You will go back and add to the sensations until you have a completed visualization. With the bicycle one, did you straighten the pedal with your toe before pushing against it to start your ride? Does the chain clank against the chain guard? Are there creases in the rubber

21

handlebar covers? Are there stiff plastic streamers of red and white coming out the ends of the rubber covers? Is the seat broad or narrow? Is this a mountain bike or an old blue Murray with twenty-four-inch wheels? The latter was my favorite childhood bike. Feel the sweat in your hands on the handlebars? Is the rubber worn thin on the ends so you can feel the metal tubing against your palms? Is the road dirt with pebbles or smooth dust? Are you on a paved bike path? Are you bouncing over rocks and jumping logs in the woods? Is it hot and sunny around you or cool and damp? Is the pavement wet and sending up splashes of water from the tires? What does the air smell like? Is there a scent of flowers or willow? Or is there a metallic odor about as you pedal past a railroad yard? Are birds chirping or are there noises of industrial sites or automobiles around you? Think about all the minute details as you proceed through a visualization exercise. Then apply this technique to your magic to make it *real* and comprehensible.

The clearer your vision of your magical goal is obtained, the more likely your success will be. All magic begins in the mind, and all that we know must first be defined by the mind to be known. This concept forms the basis for perceiving our reality, and it is also why we need to know clearly what we are trying to accomplish in performing magic. Until you can define your purpose and your objectives, knowing them as "fact obtained" is impossible. The best you can achieve is a scatter-shot approach, which amounts to a wasted effort garnering unsatisfactory results. By practicing visualizing detailed scenes, objects, or experiences, you develop that ability, and it is vital to the practice of magic.

2

Tables of Correspondences

The Book of Shadows

The basic tools for spell working include the wand, ritual knife (athame), cutting knife (bolline), candle, incense, cauldron, pentacle, a cup of beverage, bowl of salt, bowl of water, and a libation bowl, but you do not need all of these items to conduct magic. The main purpose of most of these tools is to set the mood and encourage that altered state where magical power is accessed and directed into manifestation. Indeed, you can conduct magic with concentration alone or with gestures, or using only a wand. There is one tool, however, that you create during the course of your practice that you will use repeatedly for determining the structure and components of your spells, as well as for interpreting the signs and symbols arising from your work. That tool is your Book of Shadows, commonly abbreviated as "BOS."

Many topics can be covered in a BOS, including your personal philosophy, a code of ethics, the various familiar

charges and redes of Wicca, a Wheel of the Year with discussions on the meanings of the Sabbats, a listing of tools and their uses, recipes for cakes, beverages, and meals to use in conjunction with Esbats and Sabbats, rituals for these occasions and for various Rites of Passage, runic tables and magical alphabets, special calendar days of observance, and notes on spells conducted. But perhaps most important of all, the contents of this book are the lists of correspondences you will create. You are the one who has to determine what lists you need and what you want on them.

You may find that your BOS becomes cluttered and certainly out of any type of alphabetical order as you add to it over the years, and you may find that you need more than one book. You could tab the BOS and set up a table of contents at the front, and you will know from practice what is in each book if you end up with several. Many Witches use the computer to index their BOS and keep it on disk, or use notebooks to which pages can be easily added. Having to hand-write everything is very time consuming, so word processing is often used as a substitute. Still, there is that sense of familiarity with handling your own BOS filled with your own particular style of writing. The choice is yours.

As you follow your path in the Craft, much of what you have written will become so familiar that it will not be visited much in your BOS—such as the meanings for the phases of the Moon or the interpretations of the Sabbats. Your personal lists of *correspondences*, however, will be vital to your practice. Whether handwritten or done on the computer, the purpose remains the same—to help keep your practice consistent, and to build the energies of these connections between yourself and the magic you work. The more magic you conduct with these correspondences, the easier the manifestation of the desired goal. Additionally, the more experience you gain in what works for you and what does not, the more skillfully honed will become your correspondences. Not everyone sees the same correlations, because all magic is an individual matter, but there are a number of traditionally accepted correspondences that are generally recognized among practitioners of the Craft. The fact that so many magic workers utilize the same images increases the correlation of

25

these images in the astral realm, from which then the manifestations can be drawn.

Through developing lists of correspondences, your practice becomes consistent, triggering a subconscious and astral connection between the symbolism and energies raised, in order to bring a desired goal into physical manifestation. Before anything can be created, it must first exist in the mind of the creator—in the case of spell work, the practitioner is the creator, generating the link between thought or idea, and manifestation. Correspondences function through the understanding of the individual that there are indeed different realms of existence, and that through magic, these realms can be accessed and traversed. In Appendix A, I have collated the various lists found throughout the *Green Witchcraft* series of books (*I-III*) and you may want to add these to your BOS.

Herbal Correspondences

Using herbs in spellwork adds to the energy and potency through their association with the Elementals: Earth with their roots, leaves, flowers, nuts, and berries; Air with their fragrance; Fire with their growth from sunlight and their internally affecting qualities; and Water in their growth, juices, and nourishment. The Green Craft involves a close affiliation with the Elementals as beings and *powers* (think of earthquakes, tornadoes, volcanic eruptions, and hurricanes), and the herbs are part of that kinship. Herbs are selected for the changes they are perceived to produce; for the qualities they possess, represent, or relate to you. In using herbs, you are strengthening the connection between the Elementals and the spell as well as between the Elementals and yourself. The four qualities vibrate within you and the herbs, and are focused to work in the spell by your invoking of those powers through the characteristic of the herb, directed to a specific goal as described within the framework of the spell. There are herbs that invoke and focus on the powers of the Four Elementals, and these may be used as offerings to honor these essences of life and their connection to ourselves.

In the Appendix A lists, the herbal correspondences are for magical use, **not for medical consumption**. There are many books that cover medicinal herbal use, but this is not one. My focus is magical; intended for use in the creation of spells. The lists here are by herb and uses, and by the intended purpose and those herbs that have appropriately attuned energies. There are also "Dark Power" herbs listed for magical workings focused upon the Hunter and Crone aspects of the Divine, and energies related to Underworld and Shadowland, as engaged and activated through your particular perspective.

Trees and shrubs are also part of the herbal bounty for the Practitioner. While parts of trees may be edible (walnuts and almonds) or have medicinal value (willow bark for fever), the listings in this book are for using the leaves, roots, stems, flowers, berries, nuts, or bark in various types of spell work, including charms and dream pillows. With rowan (mountain ash), very few herbalists even consider the berries for ingestion, and my mother used to caution me not to eat them. Nevertheless, the berries in small quantity have medicinal value. There are numerous guides available for herbal medicines, and it is best to review several before following any one herbal remedy.

You may want to grow your own herbs, which is relatively easy to do since most herbs are what other people might consider weeds, growing untended and wild. If you do not live near a natural supply of wild herbs, I recommend cultivating them in a sunny area unless the sun's heat in your location tends to burn out plants. In which case you might want to plant the herbs in the shade of a large tree, potted on a porch, or even indoors in containers near windows or glass doors. The soil needs, climate preferences, and watering needs are included in packaged seeds or setting plants, so you can judge what is appropriate to your yard or containers.

The other option is to buy herbs in occult supply shops, grocery stores, or as herbal teas (bulk, rather than teabags, being best). The latter may be found in health food stores and specialty shops. Fresh is best for magic as the energies are bright and alert, but you can have equal success with dried herbs, simply by calling upon the latent energies and reinvigorating them. For some types of magic, you could place dried herbs in a bowl set on the pentacle (for Earth energy) on your altar and sprinkle with charged water, calling upon the herbal energies to awaken to work with you. In other cases, the energies of dried herbs are called upon and released into action through dropping them into a candle flame, or placing them in a pouch; then they are energized through passing the pouch through the symbols of the Elementals.

Herbs should be collected on a dry day, preferably cut with your bolline or a tool used consistently for this purpose (scissors, for example, have a traditional occult association and may be magically empowered for gardening work). Select the gathering day by the phase of the Moon. Although the romantic notion of Witches collecting herbs in the dead of night by the light of the Moon is still envisioned by many, the reality is that you are taking a lot of chances trying to do this kind of work at night. If you cannot see what you are doing or what you are running into (some poor spider having worked all night may go hungry because you blundered into its giant web and destroyed it), you could end up trampling herbs, tripping over roots or the occasional wandering night creature, getting your hair tangled in tree branches, and even collecting the wrong herbs. Your level of frustration could negate all the nocturnal energies you seek to draw upon, so unless you are very familiar with the area and have a clear path to the plants, you may as well work with the daylight. Choose the timing of your collecting by the Moon phase, and perhaps by the day of the week and hour of the day. The Full Moon and Dark Moon energies remain effective in stronger or lesser degrees for three days before and after the actual date of the phase, so keep that in mind when planning your herb-collecting day. Check an astrological calendar for when the Moon is void of course, since you will want your collecting and spell work to "avoid the void" in order to retain the essential Lunar influence.

Tell the plant why you need to remove a piece of it and ask for permission. By letting the herb know your intent before you cut, the plant may indicate to you which stem, leaf, or flower it is willing to give to your purpose. Try not to take more than you need. You should either leave something in return or give the plant your blessing (extending some of your energy to the plant through your open palm). Garden plants are likely to be more generous and less interested in receiving a special gift because you are already familiar to them and your tending of them acts as a continuous gift. Nevertheless, when gathering herbs for spell work, I recommend leaving some kind of token of your appreciation behind, be it a symbol (pentagram or protective) drawn in the ground in front of or around the plant, a blessing, a coin, a bit of milk, grain (oats or wheat), or something similar.

Some of the plants listed in Appendix A are included only as a historical/literary reference, and I advise against using any poisonous plant; even touching the oils of the leaves or inhaling the smoke may be dangerous. There are plenty of substitute herbs available that are easier to work with. Some herbs, such as rue, may cause a skin irritation in sensitive people, and there are typical garden flowers that are poisonous as well, such as larkspur (in large doses) and foxglove (the powerful drug digitalis is derived from this). While there are herbs used medicinally, they may cause a reaction or serious internal organ injury if taken in quantity, such as St. Johnswort (sun sensitivity) and comfrey (liver damage). I do emphasize that these listings are magical, and are intended as a starting point for your BOS—you will naturally add to them or alter them as you grow in your practice of the Craft.

Incenses are derived from a number of the herbs, flowers, roots, and nuts listed, so you can select the herbs you want for a purpose, and match the incense and any essential oil needed accordingly. The practice of the Craft is rather like selecting choices from a menu of options. There are herbs that can be burned in a candle, stuffed into a dream pillow, added to an object, rubbed onto a tool or spell item, or sewn up into a charm. There are incenses to enhance the atmosphere for the intended purpose of the Craft work, and there are herbal (essential) oils to dress candles, tools, and objects in magical practice. Unless you prefer to create your own, these oils can be purchased in most stores. The oils will energize according to the properties of the herbs from which the oils are derived.

Using Dark Power Herbs

Many nonpoisonous herbs can be added to candle flames during spellwork, but wormwood requires good ventilation. Dark power herbs are used to honor the Sidhe, the Elementals, and the Dark Aspects of the Divine at rituals dedicated to them or seeking their aid. These herbs are also utilized in the cleansing and dedication of dark power tools, those specifically used in Dark Moon Esbats, as an example, and moving negative energies into a positive goal (as described in *Green Witchcraft II*). Depending on the purpose of the ritual or spell, these herbs may be used in pouches, pillows, charms, washes, or candle magics.

Poisonous herbs were once added to strengthen charms and spells, but since even handling some of these herbs can be dangerous as the toxins can be rubbed onto the skin or absorbed through the skin, the practice has pretty much evaporated. Herbs such as belladonna and henbane may be planted around a house to ward intruders and deflect negative or malevolent energies, but again, you have to consider the dangers to pets and children inherent with any toxic plant. There are a number of commonly used decorative plants that are poisonous; these include foxglove, holly, and oleander. While belladonna and henbane are often found naturally in untended areas, such as vacant lots and in sites being developed for new housing, cultivation as decorative plants is not a good plan, especially as even the seeds or seed pods of henbane could poison a curious child, and the berries of belladonna can cause paralysis. Part of the practice of Green Witchcraft involves observation, becoming aware of your surroundings and learning about the local natural flora and fauna, and this can be used to search out naturally occurring herbs. When selecting from Nature rather than from your own garden, be sure to take only what you need and leave behind some herbs for propagation.

Planets, Hours, and Days

Whenever possible, choose the day for your spell work based on the planetary influences on that day and how this relates to your work.

When creating spells, the days of the week can be used to enhance the power or direction of the spell. More strength can be added by attuning the day of the week with the herbs that relate to that particular day. As an example, while you could do a money spell on Monday, to get the optimal effect for your efforts you should try to align the spell casting on a day more in tune with gaining wealth, such as Thursday, with the influence of Jupiter. But if you are looking to increase income through a communicative venture, you could use Wednesday for the influence of Mercury.

Latin-based languages retain the planetary names for the days of the week (Lunes, Martes, Miercoles, Jueves, and Viernes), while the Saxon/Germanic influenced languages (such as English) have given the days of the week a more Northern/Teutonic flavor with deity names such as Woden, Thor, and Tiws (Northern version of war god, Mars), except for Saturn's day (Saturday). Sunday (the Sun's day) has in Latin cultures been reinterpreted as the God's day (Domingo)—which is appropriate for the Sun God.

The best days for dark power spells are those of Dark Sabbats, Dark Esbats, and celestial events such as eclipses and comet visits. Otherwise, the days most suitable for dark power magics are Saturday, Wednesday, and Monday. It was the positioning of the days in the week that held significance to my mother and grandmother. The first day of the week was considered to be Saturday (as is seen in calendars from Spain and Hispanic America) and sacred to the divine as Holly King, Ancient of Days, and Dark Lord. Wednesday is sacred to Annis, the Hag, Crone, and the Dark Lady. Monday is the Moon's Day and is excellent for divinations, Fairy magics, contacting the Sidhe, and working with the denizens of Otherworld.

Daily Colors and Herbs

The colors are important in the construction of spell work for their energy vibration and subconscious effect on your mind. If you have other associations for these colors, add them. The BOS is always being amended as you gain experience. Picking a color, as well as herbs, to match the day and planning your spells to take place on an appropriate day increases the power of the spell. You can fine tune it even more with day and night hours (based on sunrise and sunset) and their planetary aspects. On the run, this is not all that great a factor in spell work, but if you have the time to gather as much like-energy together for a spell, then matching the days, colors, herbs, and hours will give you a sense of structure and solidity you may require for optimal focusing. How much astrological influence you want to work with depends upon your interests. The Moon phase and the day of the week are basic in Green Craft spell work, avoiding only the Moon's void-of-course time to prevent a lessening of desired lunar energies.

Runic Tables and Divination Symbols

Typical lists of correspondences in a Book of Shadows include the magical properties, correlations, meanings, or significance of herbs, incenses, colors, crystals and stones, inscriptions (such as runic or ogham), symbols in divination, planets, days, hours, Moon phases, and Zodiac signs. These relationships are interwoven in spell crafting to create a coherent focus for magical work. Adding inscriptions derived from a sigil (from planetary squares or an alphabetical Witches' wheel), table of runes, ogham, or other alphabet with their meanings increases the focus for the energy you raise. Runes are often combined to form magical monograms attuned to a particular goal, with the last symbol inscribed acting as the *bindrune* that holds it all together. The symbols for possessions and wealth can be drawn together as a talisman, for example, and may be inscribed or painted onto an appropriate crystal or stone to carry, or onto a candle of the right color to burn for a money spell. The ogham and runes can also be used as individual symbols for their magical meaning. You can also develop your own symbols: hearts for love, a flower for joy, a dollar sign for money, an arrow for action or direction, and a tulip for friendship are some examples.

A list of symbols offers meanings for the images found in visual divinations such as might appear in tea leaves, candle wax after a spell, clouds, smoke, or dreams. There are a number of books that list meanings for symbols, particularly dream correspondences, but you will find that you will develop your own list over time. In the case of dreams, however, the individual event and symbology will be influenced by the sensations that accompany them as well as by what was on your mind at bedtime, the day's activities, or even what you ate. Your intuition will show you the source and meaning of your dreams. Trust yourself.

Stones and Crystals

The listing for stones and crystals in Appendix A will give you a means of focusing your energy through the magnifying power of these items. Meditation is one of the most power-inducing magical techniques for the Witch, and these stones and crystals enhance that power, focus it, and direct it to the objective or goal desired by the Witch, just as crystals are used to send radio signals. Crystal balls and polished obsidian work well for divinations, meditation, travel to other worlds and planes, spiritual development, and transference of energy. Some stones and crystals have multiple variations, which are listed by the color or type. *Program* a crystal by holding it to the third eye and focusing on the desired purpose you have for the crystal.

Once a crystal or gem has been charged and programmed, you can use it to create elixirs, which are energy-charged waters used as a magical wash. The energy vibrated through a crystal is affected by the Moon phase it is exposed to while soaking in a cup of spring water. You can use bottled spring water if there are no springs in your area, or well water may be used as it comes from the water table stored within the Earth. Set the stone in the water for one hour, exposed to the Full, New, or Dark Moon according to your need. A drop of brandy or whiskey can be added if desired to help "hold" the energies, but this is not essential to creating an elixir. Do a consecration ritual for the elixir by blessing the water and passing the container through the symbols of the Elementals (set on the pentacle for Earth, then pass through incense smoke, candle flame, and sprinkle the container exterior with water). Remove the crystal or stone, cleanse and store as usual. Store your elixir in a sealed (corked or lidded) jar away from direct sunlight. The elixir may be sipped for meditations as an aid to alignment of your internal energies prior to spell work, or the water may be sprinkled onto the spell-crafting materials for energy focus.

Being very functional, especially when charged by the light of the Moon, or by a cosmic event such as meteor showers and comets, stones may be utilized during spell work in numerous ways. You can select your stone by its correspondence to your purpose and goal (Appendix A), consecrate it during your spell crafting, and add it to a candle (let it rest near the wick—obviously a taper will not work for this, only votives and pillars), include it inside a dream pillow, sachet, mojo bag, medicine bag, charm, or add it to the cauldron in which you are concocting your spell. The stones may also be arranged around the spell working area, placed on the completed spell, or used as energy focusing decoration. You can let your stones and crystals rest overnight on a bed formed from a slab of amethyst crystals, or use a bowl of sea salt (found in most grocery stores close to the regular salt and spices), then store them in a dark cloth or away from light so they can regather their energies. The amethyst bed is washed in spring water or running water and turned upside down onto the crystal points to air dry. The one crystal that never needs to be cleansed, however, is danburite, which is both energizing and conducting in its own right.

The phase of the Moon may be considered for the energy properties associated with it and the crystal or stone being placed under its influence so that the two are balanced. The Full Moon is excellent for energizing any crystal or stone, but is especially conducive for clear crystals, while the New Moon is good for agates and fluorites, and the Dark Moon for obsidian and dark power stones such as chrysocolla and coral. Eclipses help to energize stones for passage between the worlds. Comets are excellent for power and energizing crystals, especially when you focus on the ancientness of the comet, its lonely travels lighting a shining path through the vast darkness of space, the changes incurred on the worlds it has passed once before, and age, timelessness, and eternity. Meteors enhance change and transformation energies.

Most people like to use one large crystal as a *generator* to recharge other crystals. The generator is one you attune to your own energies after consecration so that other stones can be realigned after use. The used stone or crystal is cleansed as previously described, but you can give it a *neutral* energy by placing it on a pentacle and setting the generator on top of it for an hour prior to storing. This *occupies* the stone and prevents stray energies from affecting it. I think of this process as similar to giving a baby a pacifier until the baby falls asleep. The stone is engaged in associating with you through the generator without actually performing a task for you. Refresh your generator periodically by setting it under the light of the Full Moon for a few hours so the crystal regenerates its power to calm and center other stones. Handle this one frequently, learning its facets and designs, traveling within, and seeing the world from the crystalline perspective. This forges a stronger link between you and the generator, and of course, the best generator is one you have respectfully addressed and that has indicated an inclination to work with you.

Preparation for Spell Work

Factors of Magic Working

The steps for conducting magic in a ritual format should be noted in your BOS, then followed as closely as possible. By using a routine consistently, you are conditioning your subconscious mind, as well as your conscious mind, that something special is about to happen. This is not to say that spur of the moment magic is not effective—it certainly is, but following a routine trains your energy flow and makes any magic working come easier. Magic is rather like learning to play the piano—while you can play tunes, your efforts will turn out better if you take the time to warm up with the scales. The more you conduct magic following a basic format, the more smoothly the energy will flow, primarily because you are not forging a new path with each endeavor. Perhaps the most difficult aspect of magical practice is the *practice*, the accustomization, as it were, of drawing upon magical energies, but once you start a routine, it becomes an amazingly natural process.

Here is a list that can be placed in your BOS as a reminder of the steps for conducting ritual magic.

1. Choose the timing of the spell
2. Outline the ritual and prepare the tools and materials
3. Purify yourself
4. Purify the working space (start of circle casting)
   a. Light altar candles and incense
   b. Sweep the circle area
5. Cast a circle (create a sacred space)
   a. Light candles at the Quarters
   b. Draw the energy boundary of the circle
   c. Asperge
   d. Cense
   e. Anoint self
   f. Call upon the Elementals
6. Invocation to the Divine
7. Perform the Ritual observance
8. Raise and direct energy
9. Ground (Earth) the residual power
10. Take some refreshment
11. Benediction to the Divine
12. Open the circle (sacred space)
    a. Farewell the Elementals
    b. Snuff the candles at the Quarters
    c. Withdraw the energy boundary of the circle

Timing Magical Workings

With most spell work, timing enhances the energy and determines the focus. In the Green Craft, the major criteria for conducting certain types of spells is the phase of the Moon. If the need is urgent, of course, any phase can be used as long as your focus takes the phase into consideration, crafting the spell to be in accord with the Moon. The Moon phases are the new crescent Waxing Moon, called the Maiden; the Full Moon, called the Mother; and the old crescent Waning Moon, called the Crone. There is also the Dark Moon, which is the hidden face of the Goddess, or the Mystic Moon. The Blue Moon is the second Full Moon in a solar month, which may be worked with for high energy or calling upon the Fair Folk for their kind influence. The Sidhe Moon (or Fairie Moon) is the second Dark Moon in the same solar month, and it opens the doorway into Otherworld and Sidhe energies. When the Moon glows a deep reddish brown it is called the Blood Moon, but as this can occur in any month, the energy is linked with the season (such as autumn and hunting) and related in an intuitive sense with the normal lunar descriptive. Lunar energies can be further defined by the zodiac sign the Moon is passing through and the relationship between the Moon and other planets, which you can get from an astrological almanac or calendar.

Just as the phases of the Moon affect the ocean tides, they also affect energy flow. The Waxing Moon of the Maiden, beginning with the thin sliver of crescent of the Moon reappearing after the Dark Moon, up until the Full Moon, is the phase for increase, of inaugurating energies, for drawing promising things and beneficial energies to you, and so is the best time for magics dealing with new beginnings or developing works; for initiating new projects and working toward a goal. This is when you do spells for gaining such things as wealth, happiness, a new job, and love.

The Waning Moon of the Crone, beginning with the diminishment after the Full Moon through to the New Moon Esbat, when there is only a thin sliver of the Moon visible prior to becoming totally dark, is best used for magical work involving banishings, purgings, or exorcisms. This is when you get rid of bad habits, or banish poverty for example. The Dark Moon is good for divination, dark power rituals, rebuilding, transformations, and spiritual meditations. Magic work is acceptable during the Dark Moon when consecrating a dark aspect tool because the very element of the mystery of that transforming instant from Tomb to Womb is being called upon. The Sidhe Moon offers another opportunity for Dark Aspect empowerment of a tool, and the Sidhe may be called upon for a consecration at this time. The Blue Moon offers an additional jolt of power to spell work, and is a good time to invite Fairies to your surroundings. The Blood Moon may be useful for successful magics relating to hunting, combat, and spells requiring aggressive energies. Focus is what matters with this Moon, so you could use this Moon to do magic that moves energy toward the aggressive accomplishment of a need, such as gaining peace in a strife-ridden area, or gaining a promotion at work. The practitioner has to determine what feels comfortable for timing.

The Full Moon of the Mother is the familiar connection to Witchcraft, being the most celebrated Esbat, and a time for honoring the Lady, revitalizing spiritual connection, and calling upon Her for instruction. This Moon offers the best energy for spells of completion, seeing the magic as done, and for honoring the Elemental energies and helpful spirits. Often a spell might start a few days before the Full Moon so that by ritually moving a candle or burning it an hour each day until the Full Moon, you see the magic as in progress until the final day on which you celebrate attainment of the desired goal. This Moon phase is also good for Initiations and Dedications, and any magic in which spiritual and magical advancement is emphasized. Here is when the ritual of Drawing Down the Moon is normally performed, bringing the lunar energy into yourself or into a container of water to charge it for use in rituals and celebrations. This same ritual may be applied to the Dark Moon as well for Dark Aspect magics (see pages 35–42 of *Green Witchcraft II*).

Planetary and celestial arrangements may be factored into the timing of your spells if you are so inclined. These include monthly astrological signs, planetary movement through the signs and houses of the Zodiac, planetary interrelationships (conjunctions, trines, squares, etc.), Mercury in retrograde (impedes communication), and lunar void-of-course (impedes emotional, intuitive, and magical energy flow). For this, an astrological planner, almanac, or calendar is most useful; then check your BOS listing of planetary associations in the planning of your spell.

Magic may also be planned according to the most propitious hour of the day or night. You already have created your planetary tables, so you can time your spells for an hour conveniently situated for your daily life and ruled by the desired planetary sign conducive to your purpose. Just as each hour of the day has a representative planet, so does each day of the week. You can optimize the energy of your spell, then, by picking the appropriate moon phase, day, and hour in which to conduct your magic.

Numerological Associations in Timing Spell Work

The number of the hour is another factor that can be utilized in spell creating. The basis lies in numerology, and if you find astrology too much trouble to deal with, the numbers of 1 through 9 work very well. When finding a suitable hour by the planetary hours chart (Appendix A), you could additionally include the numerical energy. So if the third hour after sunset is chosen for your work, and that is 9:00 P.M., you can also use the number 9 as a focal point, particularly in binding a spell to completion or new path energy, as an example. When not using the planetary hours chart, you could go by the number of the day, or by the number of the hour. Combinations in which the same number is repeated reinforce the power of that number, such as casting a career spell in the third month of the year and on the third day of the week, at 3:00 P.M. Planetary correlations are not involved here, only the numbers, yet the influence of Jupiter lies inherent in the number three, as does the triple aspect, and the summation of numbers as nine, which binds the energies to a completion.

Besides the magical import and planetary alignment, numbers may also be used in relation to the Elementals and to the letters of the alphabet. Personal focus is the key factor in determining how much of the number correlations you envision. The alphabet letters and their number correspondence are included in the Appendix A numerology list. You can reduce any proper noun, name, or word into a numerical unit by noting the assigned number for each letter, adding them up, then reducing the sum to a final single digit number by adding those numbers together. This is useful for seeing the relationship between your birth date number, birth name/wedded name numbers, and address number. In other words, you can work at bringing your life into alignment by matching your address, as an example, with your birth or name number. When creating your Craft Name, you can align the numerical energies by using a name that has the same value as your birth/legal name for balance. Or you can create a name whose combined letters result in the numerical magical meaning you desire to emphasize in yourself, thus drawing more of this particular energy to yourself. By combining all of these interpretations into one listing, you keep your BOS less cluttered and have easy access to the related information. The influence of the number is listed in the chart, so you would match your magical purpose with the energy of a number and develop your spell to embrace this number.

Using Numerology

You can choose your timing, materials, or process according to numerical influences. Thus, you could use the date, or the month and date, or the month, date, and year to focus on a number appropriate to your needs. In finding the base number of 1 to 9, you add together the digits and reduce these to a final, single digit. If the day of the week is 15, you could see the numerical energy is that of the number 6, and so could be used in decision-making. If you want to do a spell, but timing by the astrological hours is not convenient (let us say that your optimal spell hour is 1 A.M., but you have to go to work at 6 A.M. and do not want to stay up that late) then you can conduct the spell instead by the numerological meaning. Thus, looking for a time after sunset, you could focus on the energy value of the number itself (sunset at 6 P.M., spell at 9 P.M. for Energy) rather than upon the planetary correspondence.

The numbers are intended to aid in your focus on the type of energy you want to raise and direct, so you can create your own parameters for finding the right number. If the date of 15=6=energy for decision-making fits your spell purpose, then this is all you need. You do not need to factor in the month (8 for August, as an example), which would change the reduced number from 6 to 5 (15 as 1+5=6; that 6, plus 8 for the month makes 14, and 1+4=5). You set up the framework in your mind for how much numerology you want to focus on—hour, date, month, year—according to what gives you the number with the associated desired energy. This is simply another method of energy manipulation, which is an integral part of magic. Practice making numerical associations; find your destiny number by adding the numbers of your birth date (month as numbers 1–12, date, and year) and see how much of your sur-roundings and activities reflect your destiny number, or how you can bring these into alignment with that number.

Two-digit numbers are used for mystical value, the most popular being 13 as the perfect number of the Creatrix Goddess who is the Triple Goddess, or of the number for All (1) and the Trinity (3). Other numbers are 10 for completion, 12 for the even dozens and as the two triple-aspected deities (Triple Goddess and Triple God) together, 3+3=6, but then you can multiply the 6 aspects by 2 for the God and the Goddess as both separate (3+3=6) and united as One (6) to get 12. It is all a matter of mind-set. Fairy magics also are traditionally related to the number 12. Multiple numbers like 11, 22, 33, 44, and so forth offer double emphasis of the main number. Sometimes the doubles are read as 2 by 2 or 3 by 3, etc. for a bal-ance (2 energy) of the value of the number. Triple numbers are used for bindings; quadruple numbers are used for squaring and set-ting—making the value of the number a foundation (4) for a spell. These multiples are used mainly in knot magics, wherein each knot tied binds the energy of the spell. Referring to your BOS is how you put all the goodies together to make your spell stew, so do not worry about memorization—the correlations will come to mind intuitively as you become more accustomed to working in a particular pattern.

While Green Witchcraft is easily practiced with a focus on the phases of the Moon and the Sun rather than to planetary arrangements, astrology can be incorporated, especially if there is something happening among the planets—if there are celestial events that you feel can be attuned to your magical work. Numerological associations are more frequently used in the Green Craft. Obviously, you have more leeway in formulating spells when you can time your magic according to moon phase, hour of the day, day of the week, and the numbers of the date in any combination. Moon phases are easily adapted to your workings by focusing on the energy of that phase and creating wordings that use the phase to your advantage. For timing with the planetary hours guide that you create for your BOS from Appendix A, all you need is the time for sunrise and sunset on your spell day in your location. This information can be found in the daily newspaper, almanacs, and The Weather Channel.

If you are working magic on the East Coast directed to a place on the West Coast, you could word your spell to travel with the Sun and implement at the same hour on that coast (which would be three hours later). Play around with timing and have fun with your Craft. In this way, you will learn what circumstances are most in tune with your energy flow, where you have strengths and weaknesses, and where you need to work on developing energy. Crystals can help you bolster those weak spots so that you come to practice magic readily, no matter what the hour or the Moon phase, simply by manipulating the flow to achieve your goals.

Working with the Elementals in the Green Craft, with the Sun and Moon focus, may also involve focusing on the Elementals in their seasonal, or Quarterly, correspondences, called *Tides*. This means that you work with the energies of the year as divided into four segments through Equinoxes and Solstices. You may want to note these times in your BOS for reference, and incorporate the tides whenever possible, particularly in long-term projects. There is a BOS listing in Appendix A that may be used as an aid for Elemental references.

The first Tide incorporates Yule and Imbolc, the second has Ostara and Beltane, the third includes Litha and Lughnassadh, and the fourth encompasses Mabon and Samhain. Think, then, in terms of these Sabbat energies with the Tides. The use of West as rest and passage is reflected in various ancient traditions as the West (land of the sunset) being the direction of death and repose. The Egyptians and the Celts both used this association, and it has followed into Witchcraft. But West is also cleansing, emotions, and learning (on either a soul or lifetime level), and North is seen as the realm of the Crone, and thus of wisdom and death passage. The North tends to be seen more as a realm representing the active transition between life and death, while the West is the realm of repose in death, preparing for the next life passage, thus assessing the previous life and determining what soul-quest to strive for in the next incarnate life.

The easiest way to remember the Tides is with the seasonal connection to directions. North generally evokes an image of cold and night; therefore, Winter through Spring. East generally evokes an image of fresh air and a warming sunrise; therefore, Spring through Summer. South generally evokes an image of heat and full sunlight; therefore, Summer through Autumn. West generally evokes an image of dampness and cooling sunset; therefore Autumn through Winter.

As an example of how you could time a spell, let us say you want to increase money flow to you. From your list of correspondences, you see that the day of the week for riches is Thursday, ruled by Jupiter. Jupiter on Thursdays rules the first and eighth hour after sunrise and the third and tenth hour after sunset. The number three is a Jupiter number, so for triple potency, you would want to use a Thursday, the third hour after sunset, during a waxing moon, to perform a money spell. Let us say that on this day the sun sets at 6:00 P.M. The spell would be conducted at 9:00 P.M. (third hour after sunset), and you include in your focus the energy and power of the number 9 (from 9:00), which is 3x3, and may be used as a chanting method of binding a spell to completion. While your timing is set for optimum results, you may want to include the Elemental Tide, depending on the time of year you are in. You could perform this spell during the Air Tide for new beginnings, or Fire Tide for accomplishment and harvest, as examples. Since Jupiter rules the Fire sign of Sagittarius, you may want to opt for the Fire Tide for a maximal alignment of energies. The important thing to remember here is that ritual magic may be as complex or as simple as you want it to be—as best works for *you*.

With the Elemental Tides in mind, then, consecration of a dark aspect tool intended for use in dark power rituals and meditations, travels to Otherworld and Underworld travel, and spirit communication, would be best performed during a Dark Moon Esbat, particularly in October for proximity to Samhain, or the other dark months of September and November. While spell-casting magic is not normally performed during the Dark Moon because the mythology suggests that the God is withdrawn into the Goddess in her aspect of the transformative tomb/womb, the time is excellent for preparing a black mirror or other scrying tool.

Ritual Preparations

To create your ritual, refer to your BOS list of correspondences, choosing the elements of your spell. This is like composing a meal, selecting the components for the different courses to arrive at a palatable whole. Here is where you choose the ingredients of your spell, matching the need to what you have available. With correspondences, you look at the herbs, stones, and colors that apply to your need, as an example, then see what you actually have, and pick one or two items for your spell. Using timing considerations, you decide the avenue of approach to your magical working. Will you do a candle-burning spell (very common in Witchcraft), an amulet (such as a protection herb bag for the car), a talisman (such as a stone selected for its magical meaning, inscribed with an appropriate rune or sigil, and carried as a charm), a poppet (such as fashioning a doll for healing), or brew (such as making an elixir or magical tea)? Will you do a written spell to be burned? Or will you do a spell of increase by planting a magic-imbued seed? As you go through the possibilities, adding in the right herbs, appropriate color of candles, proper symbols, and determined timing, you ready the spell and decide what aspect of the Divine you will call upon for assistance, or if using the non-religious style of practice what aspect of Nature or the Elementals you will invoke. Write down what you plan to do, including a chant or word formula for empowering and sending the spell to do its job.

Preparation for the magic means that you are setting up all your needed tools and ingredients, and getting the work space in order. If using an altar arrangement, clean the altar, set a cloth on it, and only the equipment you need for the spell and ritual. Be sure to include the beverage and snack for invocation ritual and grounding after the spell is done. Review your notes to be sure you have not forgotten something. There is nothing quite as distracting as to be halfway through spell and realize that the pen and bottle of dove's blood ink is in the drawer in another room. While not a tremendous problem, it does mean interrupting the spell, making a doorway in the circle, leaving, returning, re-sealing the circle, and picking up from where you left off—and by then, how much energy has been dissipated? A lot of magic energy is generated by the mood you set in your circle, and so stopping midstream to do something can cause you to lose the momentum of the mood you have so carefully constructed. It is rather like bringing the subconscious mind to the foreground, only to have it shunted back as the conscious mind remembers a missing detail.

After you have everything set in place for your ritual, you need to prepare yourself for the event. The true action of personal preparation lies in the grounding and centering already discussed, but there are additional ways to get your whole body into the mood for magic work. Taking a warm bath, with herbs in a muslin or cheesecloth bag added to the water, gives you an all-over sensation of something special about to take place. Choose the herbs for your bath by the attributes you desire to express: cleansing qualities (such as lavender), magical influence (such as mugwort for lunar power, cypress for inspiration, or elderflower for consecration), energy-raising ability (such as cinquefoil or verbena), and so forth. You are cleansing yourself of the stress and cares of daily life and releasing negative or chaotic energies into the soothing waters which will then flow down the drain, taking all tension and distractions away from you.

To make an herbal bath, combine the minced leaves/flowers in a jar, then place two or three tablespoons inside the drawstring bag. Tie it off and place inside the tub as you fill it with water. You may want to add salt for purification baths. Herbal baths for connecting with Nature may consist of combinations of chamomile, clove, heather, hops, lavender, lemon balm, marigold, mint, pansy, rose, rosemary, and savory.

During the bath is when I like to enter into a light meditative state. I begin by slowly taking a deep breath, slowly exhaling, repeating this, letting the clutter of daily thoughts slip from me, dismissing distracting thoughts while I focus on the aroma of the herbs, the here and now of infusing magical energy. I can then move into a simple breathing exercise, inhaling to the mental count of two, holding for one count, and exhaling for two counts, until I feel totally at peace. You can consciously let the stress gather in your shoulders, then release it to flow from your fingertips into the water, while the herbal packet may be brushed along your face, shoulders, and arms to act as an aura cleanser. A light meditation keeps you aware of your surroundings while helping to develop your creative ability and aiding in the centering process. It provides you with the opportunity to visualize the magical process in a calm atmosphere so you can see how a spell will work.

The bathing process assists the mental transition from ordinary to magical, and sets the mind to a manifestation context. This mindset can be called into play as you bathe or dry off, as you robe or begin lighting incense and candles in the ritual area—it evolves naturally from your grounding and centering so that you can connect with all aspects of the earth as part of a cohesive entity—animal, mineral, plant, water, clouds, sky. Meditation becomes a primary step to your union with the cosmos and to the planes of energy so that you can reach out to these and draw upon their power in your work. Your awareness is opened to achieve alternative states of being before you have even begun the spell work, so now you are ready to conduct magic.

You may follow the Circle Casting Ritual in Appendix B or create your own, following the guidelines previously given. Not everyone raises a candle at the Quarters to invoke light and the Elemental aspect to the circle: to illuminate and strengthen at the North; illuminate and enliven at the East; illuminate and warm at the South; and to illuminate and cleanse at the West. Also, not everyone lights a candle at the Quarters, each one being a color appropriate to the Elemental: green (or brown) for Earth; yellow (or light blue) for Air; red (or orange) for Fire; dark blue (or seagreen) for West. For emphasis of occasion, you might want to make all the Elemental candles a related color (such as shades of purple for spiritual work, black for protection work, or white for purification/general ritual work).

You could choose not to use candles at all for Elemental markers, replacing them with symbolic objects relating to yourself more personally. If you are a gardener, different aspects or tools could be used: a dish of potting soil for Earth, seed for Air, a kiln-fired clay pot for Fire, and a watering can for Water. I encourage creativity and changes that you can relate intuitively to because the appeal of ritual varies with each person—and, especially with ritual magic, you must be able to relate to and direct the energy that you raise. If using stones or crystals instead of candles to mark the Quarters, make associations with color or type. Crystals and gems can be laid out according to color or feeling: green tourmaline for Earth, fluorite or clear crystal for Air, carnelian for Fire, and beryl or lapis lazuli for Water. Stones could be representational with granite or petrified wood for Earth, geode or white marble for Air, pumice or lava for Fire, and river rock or sandstone for Water. You could use different objects for each Quarter—shell, nut, stone, feather, lava chunk, fired clay, brick—as long as you can distinguish an Elemental pattern.

MANIPULATING
MAGICAL ENERGY

Working with Energy

The purpose for the circle cast during spell work is to contain the energy you are raising until you are ready to let it flow to complete a task. The circle is not a flat spot on the ground around you, but should be envisioned as a sphere that passes through walls and floors, under the ground and through the air above to encapsulate the magic worker. Once the raised energy is sent, the circle can then be opened. By meditating prior to your circle casting, you switched off the routine consciousness that chatters in your head in endless circles of fear, guilt, anger, or recrimination, and rehashing of events that had a negative effect on your mental and emotional health. This switching off allows your subconscious mind, your intuitive Self, to take over, moving you into that alternative state that gives you a new, cosmic perspective. The circle is drawn, the Elementals are called upon, a candle is lit, incense is burning, and the act of grounding and centering works as a small meditational procedure

directed at preparing you for enacting a magical ritual. But to perform even that most basic magical practice—grounding and centering—you must be able to manipulate energy in a magical manner.

The purpose of visualization exercises is to prepare you for just this type of energy work. If you cannot see or sense the energy around you and in you, then working on your visualization skills should help. Think of this as a highly detailed style of daydreaming. When you were a child, did you ever pretend to be someone or something other than who or what you are? Were you a horse, dog, dragon, unicorn, or superhero? How did you envision yourself? How did you feel about yourself? This is the sort of natural developmental stage of growing up, called role playing or modeling, during which a child tries on different personas until finding one that feels comfortable—at least that is the ideal, but often, the child is merely accepting an unfulfilling role imposed upon him or her by family, peers, society, culture, or religion. With Witchcraft, you are reclaiming the power to manipulate energy to attain the role that *you* choose for yourself, and that is one reason why you must be able to visualize and work with energy.

There are different ways of *seeing* energy. Some people are more intuitive and sense it, while others are more visual and sight it as a glow or haze of different colors. Auras are energy fields extruding around matter and may be sighted as a shimmering light or as colors depending on the object and the person viewing it. Often the auric layer closest to the body is the easiest to see, appearing as a thin outline of the object or person, sometimes seen as a shadow. Beyond that, the aura spreads into a wider band that is bordered with a diffused glow, which may take on color tones indicative of mood, health, or emotional state. This wider aura may not be seen visually, but felt or sensed, as when you just know not to bother someone because he or she *appears* grumpy, ill, out of sorts, or barricaded.

For learning to sense energy, you might want to start by working to identify the main chakra energies of your own body. Although the chakra system is from India, my mother passed along to me a very similar concept without specific names (see Class 6, *Green Witchcraft III*), so that I knew about these centers and the activation

53

and balancing of the energies without actually calling them chakras or the kundalini. Today the chakras are more familiar, and these seven power centers (with the terms my mother used as I was growing up put in parentheses), are located at the base of the spine (anal and genital area), the sacral plexus (abdomen), the solar plexus (stomach), the heart (same), the throat (same), the third eye (brow), and the crown (top of the head). The colors associated with these sites are red, orange, yellow, green, blue, purple, and white (there are some variations on this, with the base or root chakra sometimes designated as black or brown).

Awakening these energy sites is described as rousing the sleeping snake or serpent of the kundalini, which is a powerful opening of psychic awareness not recommended without careful preparation. I was taught that the soles of the feet and the palms of the hands were also important energy points, associated with the Elementals: left foot Earth, right foot Air, right hand Fire, and left hand Water. This is the pentagram, as well, with the head representing the Spirit and Cosmic Connection, for here is where the brain, acting as a great battery, generates mental impulses of energy. My mother felt that the energies of other people were easily accessed in this area, and the source of headaches was contact with an overload of negative energies generated by others and the brain becoming overworked while attempting to equalize the flow throughout the body. She also warned against placing the palms on the top of the head while relaxing as this impeded healthy energy flow and stunted spiritual growth. Today, people talk about stress and recognize the unhealthy problems associated with it as the tension moves out of the head region (headache and migraine), into the muscles (neck pain, stiffness, and soreness), and body organs (palpitations, heartburn, upset stomach, and colitis). Stress and anxiety will throw all your chakras out of balance, and so a meditative realignment of energy is the first step to recovery.

To work with energy, you should become familiar with your own energy centers. Try sitting comfortably on the floor or on a cushion, and envisioning a swirl of colored light at each of these bodily sites. If the colors seem muddy or the movement disorganized, bring the white light from the top of your head (where your energy meets that of the cosmos) down through each of your centers to energize, brighten the colors, and regulate the spin. If the colors need darkening or adjusting, you can also visualize the energy of opposite colors working to attain a suitable tone: red with green, orange with blue, yellow with purple. You should regularly check your own energy centers and bring them into balance to stay in peak physical and mental form.

Focusing inward, trying to move your conscious center from head to belly is another exercise in learning to move energy and awareness. This is a way to prepare for astral travel and for merging meditations (transporting yourself into another object or being, such as a bird, and seeing yourself and your surroundings from that perspective—for more information, see chapter 9 of *Green Witchcraft II*). It also trains your subconscious mind to understand energy fluctuations through the movement process.

Looking for auras can be practiced simply by gazing at an object, then looking away and *seeing* it again in detail. For seeing energy fields, you may find it is easier when the subject is in front of a dark or light background—it varies for people. Practice on yourself to get started, seeing your own energy field in a mirror. Then turn your attention to other things, such as trees and plants. When gathering herbs for spells, I had earlier mentioned asking the plant for permission and sensing if the plant offered a particular portion for your use. This is a type of energy reading, so do not feel disappointed if you do not visually see auras and energy fields if you can sense them—you may simply not be a visual person. Psychic awareness comes in many forms, from audio (external or internal) to visual (external or internal) to empathic, and most people possess at least one of these abilities, and may develop it and add others through practice. Your ability to see auras may also depend on the background, so do try experimenting with a dark or a light backdrop. The inner aura is usually easiest to see, then an outer layer, broad and possibly colorful, white, or dark. For magical workings, the colors are fairly much the same as per the list of correspondences, with the exception that dark areas may need energy input (crystal therapy helps).

When you ground and center, you are feeling the energy within yourself calming and gathering. Then you are sensing the energy of the Earth as a living organism beneath your feet, and drawing that energy up through the soles of your feet into your body to intertwine with your own energies. If you do magic work without this important connection, you are essentially siphoning off your own energy, which can be debilitating and leave you open to physical and psychological illness. The connection with the Earth is extremely important. More energy may be drawn within through the cosmic connection at the crown (the top of your head). Body heat, which is an indicator of your energy, is most easily transmitted or lost through the top of the head, the soles of the feet, and the palms of the hands, thus you need to keep these well covered in cold, raw weather with wool socks, mittens, and hat so as not to deplete your energy reserves and body warmth.

It may be helpful to envision the source of the Earth energy as coming from the living planet, Gaia, of which we are a part, or as from magma, which is the molten lava core of the planet. If you do not feel the connection of energy from the Earth, again, practice your visualization skills or work with other sensing techniques. One way to practice is to rub your hands together, move them apart, then slowly bring the open palms closer together until you feel the resisting energy between them. This is a method of rousing your energy prior to cleansing someone's aura with palms passed over the aura, without touching the person, so that the aura is smoothed out from head to foot. The hands are then shaken and the palms are touched to the ground to drain out the static energy removed from the auric field. Another technique is to sit comfortably on the ground outside and hold your palms level over the ground, lowering your hands until you feel the Earth's energy pushing back up against your palms. Focus on the Earth energy and draw it up into your palms. Now focus on your own energy, and push it into the ground. You are trading energies here, rather like taking a shower, and keep manipulating the energy back and forth until you equalize it by pressing your palms to the ground and pushing out excess energy. Follow all your exercises with something to eat and drink.

With grounding and centering, you are more than sensing the energy, you are deliberately drawing it into yourself, rather like recharging a battery, in preparation for an outpouring of energy. Magical work is mainly effected by the gathering, manipulation, and transference of energy, so being able to feel the energy is a key to a successful practice. You gather your own energy together within and shoot the excess, nervous, tense energies out of the soles of your feet or your palms to be dissipated by the Earth. As soon as you are in balance, you pull fresh energy up from the Earth through your feet and feel it climb up your legs to wind itself around your spine, weaving itself with your own energy.

Using Gestures

The hands are a primary tool for moving energy, even when using wands or athames, since these are hand-held. The right hand is used to draw in Elemental Fire for energizing and empowering your magic, while the left hand is used to draw in Elemental Water to soothe, protect, and urge matters to completion. Together they invoke, unite, and bless. Gestures, then, play an important role in the visualizing of energy in motion for spells and other magical workings. The feet are involved in energy raising as well, with the left foot both drawing up the strength and power of Elemental Earth to be utilized in your workings, and the right foot gathering the spiritual, mental, and psychic energies of Elemental Air to be transmuted into physical manifestation through magical work.

Unity may be expressed by gesturing with palms outward, gathering in energy from the air as you turn the hands, palms inward, drawing your palms to your chest, blending the energies with your own, then thrusting your hands back outward in front of your body with the heels of your palms down, fingertips up, and pushing outward. You may use this gesture once (unity), twice (balance), or thrice (completion), which is one way of incorporating numerology during ritual and beginning or concluding spell work. This type of gesturing may be performed during the calling of the Quarters as part of the circle-casting ritual, and during the invocation of the Lady and the Lord.

Both hands may be used to focus raised energy into a palpable ball which is then pushed into a spell object, such as a candle, an herbal packet, a poppet, a charm, or other item. The energy may also be pushed in the general direction that a spell is to work. As an example of this, should you be working a spell and the object is in another part of the country, you *send* the energy in the direction where the object of the spell is located. I have done this sort of spell work (for healing) and as I snuffed the candle in the cauldron, watched as blue light sped around the lip of the cauldron to shoot off and disappear in the indicated direction. This was not flame, mind you, but very visible energy.

The hands are also used in Sabbat rituals, particularly to indicate the Goddess (palms up, arms spread) and the God (palms directed inward, arms crossed to the chest) in the solar phases of passage (Lughnassadh, Mabon, Samhain). Drawing blessings and Divine energy into yourself utilizes this palms inward/against the chest gesture, which is then followed by the hands motioned away and with palms down, then outward, thus releasing excessive energies. By bringing your arms and hands into a position that resembles a teepee over your head (heel of palms nearly touching, center of palms angled back, and fingers bent inward—rather like a blossom or bowl), you access Universal energy for an invocation. Proceed with the invocation, then bring your hands down on either side of your head, palms up, until level with your shoulders. This stance draws the Divine energy into balance with your own on the psychic (third eye chakra) and cosmic (crown chakra) energies, thus augmenting these receptive power centers. You may hold this position while continuing with your invocation, then move on into the hands against the chest then motioned outward to complete the cycle. You are now linked with Divine energy for magical work of any kind. When completed, ground the residual energy to be used wherever the Earth has need.

In spell work, once the energy is drawn within, directed into the spell materials, then released to accomplish the work, the palms are touched to the earth (or floor) to ground the residual energy, letting it drain out. You must learn to sense when enough is released— again, Witchcraft is an art as well as a religion, and you learn through practice. If the palms are held too long to the ground, more energy is drained than needed, and you will feel depleted. The cure for that is to ground and center, then balance the chakras, bringing up energy through each site, taking what you need, and releasing the excess into the ground—presumably with more care this time. Taking something to eat and drink will also help revitalize you while bringing you back into a routine consciousness.

Raising Energy

In all magical practice, you are accepting that all things are interconnected in the same existence. Thus, you want to "be careful what you do" because "what you send comes back" in one form or another, simply because we are all interlinked. This is where the creativity you have nurtured through meditation and visualization comes to the fore. If you are working with the Dark Aspects of the Goddess and the God—Crone and Hunter, or Lady and Lord of the Underworld—you could follow a reverse methodology that brings balance and wholeness by drawing in and redirecting the powerful dark (chaos) energy existing around you.

Your timing would be during the waning or dark phase of the Moon or an event such as an eclipse, with all the timing components matched as shown previously. If doing a banishment spell, again, you are focusing and directing the negative energies around you rather than drawing up negative energies for the work. A banishment spell, or any other waning-phase magical work, presumes the presence of negative energies already, so raising the energy is not an issue, only how to send it away in a beneficial manner.

If you feel that a lot of negative energy has accumulated around you, meditation on the reason for this will help you discover the source and how to deal with it, change it, or redirect it. Ask the Universe why this energy came to you, where it came from, how you can benefit from it, and what you really want? These are all good questions for determining your reaction to the negativity around you. Negativity is not necessarily *bad* for you—balance requires a blending of both positive and negative energies. This is the type of energy that spurs you into action, that opens up your creative impulses, and that generates a lateral thinking that takes you off the beaten path to discover new thought patterns and make the intuitive leap that results in new ideas.

Sometimes, negative energy appears to be the result of anger, but the source is most likely quite different, with anger being only a symptom. It is when you start to examine your reactions that you find what internal working is actually responsible for drawing dark power to you. But this energy is ready for you to direct, and once the source is identified, affords you an opportunity for cleansing and comforting.

Working with the positive energies is the most common style of magical practice, particularly used in the waxing and full phase of the Moon. Here is when you raise Earth energies or Universal energies for a particular task. I do want to stress that *raising* energy is vital to magical work. You do not want to direct your own personal energy into spell work simply because you will drain yourself and this can lead to illness, lethargy, and depression. This is why grounding and centering is so very important in magical practice— you are supplementing your own energies with those drawn from the vast reserves within the Earth. And since all energy runs in cycles, once the task is accomplished, that which was directed returns to the Earth to be used again. Energy, after all, cannot be destroyed, only altered. When you ground and center, you are dipping into a reservoir of energy, taking what you need to direct, releasing back the excess, and therefore temporarily augmenting without diminishing your own energy levels.

In the Green Craft, energy is worked through the individual. You are bringing Earth energies inside to blend with your own and sending it to perform a task and dissipate afterwards. This is why the Green Witch is Earth-centered. You can also bring inside the energies of the cosmos, simply because the Earth (and thus you) is part of the cosmos—the Universe is not something separate from us. The major focus, however, is through Earth-drawn energy. Universal energies come through the crown of the head, and are generally accessed for balancing and cleansing the chakras, and for spiritual connection with the Divine. Earth energies are drawn up through the feet for directing into spell work. So Earth energy is more frequently used in material magic, and Universal energy is more frequently used in personal and spiritual development magic. The ceremonial magician differentiates these, calling the first *low* magic and the latter *high* magic, but tends to assume that the Witch only operates in the field of material (low) magic. The reality of the Green Craft is that *both* magics draw upon Divine power of the immanent God and Goddess, and only the purpose or direction differs—hence, all magic is activated through Divine energy, which is why you must be careful in what you do (*"An it harm none, do what you will"*—Wiccan Rede).

After you ground and center (drawing up and intermingling energy) your connection with the Earth is open, and you are then able to raise more energy in a variety of ways to make it available for your spell work. You do not raise energy until your spell item has been completely prepared, set to be empowered, for you are now gathering together the energy needed for activation. Once gathered, the energy needs to be released in one quick jolt, so be sure your spell is completely ready before you begin raising the energy.

Dancing around your circle, with arms raised and palms open is one way to gather in the energy. With a group doing a coven spell, hands clasped or opened, as the members dance as a circle will raise a cone of energy at the center of the group for directing by the leader. But in Solitary, or personal, magical workings, you are drawing the energy to yourself for direction rather than at the center of the circle.

Another method of raising energy is to chant, usually a short rhyme that pertains to your spell. Most witches compose their own simple rhymes or chants that maintain a beat or rhythm. This chant should incorporate images that are relevant to you, and is repeated while building in sound and tempo, to raise energy and enhance the spell.

Dancing and chanting are often combined, so keep the rhyme short and to the point. If doing a positive energy spell, dance *deosil* (clockwise) around the circle. For magic using negative energy, dance *widdershins* (counterclockwise) around the circle. In the case of positive energy, you are increasing the amount you drew in from the Earth, and you keep up the dance until you feel the energy is as strong as you can handle, vibrating and ready to be released. With negative energy, you are gathering the existing surrounding energy into a compressed field, enveloping yourself with the energy condensed so you can grasp it for release.

Another type of chant used to raise energy is the traditional Witch's Rune. Here you could alter the words or frame the images in your own perception to be more in tune with your path. It is intended to be mystical and utilizes *names of power* as used in ceremonial magic. The rune itself is actually a combination of ceremonialism and the Gardnerian Tradition, but you can alter it to fit your personal viewpoint and spiritual path, invoking the deities and powers you relate to, while still following the guideline. This chant is often used in conjunction with dancing around the circle, giving you the energy of the chant as well as of the dance. You may repeat the phrases that especially appeal to you until you are ready to send the energy.

Eko, Eko Azarak
Eko, Eko Zamilak
Eko, Eko Cernunnos
Eko, Eko Aradia.
Darksome night and shining moon
East, then South, then West, then North
Harken to the Witches' Rune
Here I come to call thee forth
Earth and Water, Air and Fire
Wand and pentacle and sword
Work ye unto my desire
Hearken ye unto my word
Cord and censer, scourge and knife
Powers of the Witches' blade
Awaken all ye unto life

Come ye as the charm is made.
Queen of heaven, Queen of hell,
Horned Hunter of the night
Lend your power unto my spell
And work my will by magic rite
By all the power of land and sea
By all the might of moon and sun
As I do will, so mote it be
Chant the spell and be it done
Eko, Eko Azarak
Eko, Eko Zamilak
Eko, Eko Cernunnos
Eko, Eko Aradia.

Repeat the ending Ekos until sufficient energy is raised. Some words need to be understood in Witch terms, so *heaven* is seen as Divine connection with the Universe, and *hell* is the realm of the Goddess Hel, also known as Underworld or the Land of Shadows, thus you may envision the Goddess in her aspects of Creatrix and Crone.

The scourge is a soft "cat of nine tails," usually of velvet, used in some but not all Traditions. The background for this device in Wicca can be traced to the murals depicting the stages of initiation into a resurrection religion, most likely that of Dionysos, at the Villa of Mysteries in Pompeii, and to the convent and monastic customs of the Christian *flagellates*, still seen today in Spain during Holy Week in Seville. The original intent was to draw blood, scourging out the past life to prepare a person for entry into a new one, but this is not the practice in Wicca, being only symbolic rather than painful. The Pompeii ritual brought about an altered state as the initiate was taken through the stages of death and rebirth, demonstrating the mystery of life as an eternal cycle wherein the immortal soul is reborn, thus the practice is more suited to spiritual rather than to material magic. The Christian purpose of scourging was to mortify the flesh in a demonstrative rejection of the life, thus proving worthy for entry to the Kingdom of God, and so this is also intended as spiritual magic.

The word "eko" may have evolved from the medieval memory of the cry of the Pagan Bacchantes (maenads) of Bacchus (Dionysos), "Evoa," meaning "Thou art invoked," which was popular into the sixth century C.E. The names of power, many drawn from medieval grimores written by ceremonial magicians, may be used if they work for you. The names have been drawn from a variety of sources, including lists of angels, demons, powers, and a number of spirits imbued with planetary, elemental, and Olympic energies, but many were made up in a frenzy of energy-raising similar to the phenomenon of speaking in tongues. Connections to Fairie, Otherworld, or Heaven were indicated by placing an "ie" at the ending of a name, while an "el" ending associated the name with the Mesopotamian word for God. Still other names of power were derived by transforming Pagan deities into demons, or by using Latinized nouns as proper nouns, thus "wisdom" became the name Hagenti; Stolas came from herbs and standing stones. Again, Migene González-Wippler is a good source for information on these names of power.

Cernnunos and Aradia are Pagan deities: the Celtic Horned God and the daughter of the Moon Goddess, Diana from the Italian Strega tradition that names Aradia as the Goddess of the Witches. Other deities called the Goddess of the Witches are Hecate, Cerridwen, and Bendidia. The names of Azarak and Zamilak are given different meanings, depending on the source, but I feel that the first one might be traced to the angel of death in Jewish tradition, and the second could have been derived from the Persian Earth God, Zam. Some Traditions use the spelling "Zomelak," but even Doreen Valiente, who penned the popular Rune along with Gerald Gardner, did not know the meanings of the words, and only assumed them to be deity names (see the footnote on page 44, *A Witches' Bible*, Janet and Stewart Farrar, Phoenix Publishing Inc., 1996 edition). As long as the words work for you, with the meaning coming from your subconscious, the actual derivation may not be all that important to you—the feel is what matters.

Another way to raise energy is through manipulating your breathing. Chanting may be part of this process, and breathing obviously factors into the chanting with the growing crescendo of the chant, but a chant is not necessary for breath work. To make use of the breathing technique, simply alter your breathing pattern. You may utilize short, sharp intakes of breath, one large intake, hold, then release as you focus and direct the energy. The key to this type of energy raising is to know when to stop. Too much breath alteration, such as with panting, can make you light-headed and faint.

A sweeping type of inhaling will help gather in energy rather like a vacuum cleaner. This entails motion, generally from right to left and back again, while you envision your breath looped as a cosmic *lemniscate* (Infinity symbol—a figure 8 on its side). This is followed with a sharp, rapid exhaling directly onto the spell object. You are drawing up cosmic energy, blending it with your Earth-enhanced internal energy, and releasing this energy onto a spell item, such as a charm or talisman, for enlivening. In this instance, the breath is visualized as *breath of life* energy. There are those who feel candles used in ritual should only be snuffed or pinched rather than blown out at the end of spell work, and depending on the size of the flame, this may be practical advice. However, breath can also be seen as a way to send the energies off with a gentle power from within, rather like a kiss. In that case, blowing out a candle is acceptable, but be focused on the candle flame when you do this, not distracted and rushed. When any breath work is finished, definitely touch the ground and move into Cakes and Wine—drink a beverage and have something to eat.

Focusing, Directing, and Sending Raised Energy

Now that you have raised the energy for your spell, you do not want to lose that momentum. Planning is necessary because once the energy is raised, it must be released to do the task assigned. The focusing, directing, and sending of raised energy flows as one fluid motion, but the import of each phase combines in this action. One of the spell-planning activities is to select a word or thought image that will act as the focus of your energy raising, so that once you feel the energy is at its peak, that single word can be spoken or that image can be brought emphatically to mind. The word may be whispered, hissed, growled, shouted, or stated, but be careful not to let it escape out of the sides of the mouth. It is one thing to hiss, another to vent, so if you cannot tell the difference, use another voice technique. While a short phrase can also be used, you will dissipate some of the power raised if you take too long explaining what you want the energy to accomplish.

Directing the energy is done when the magic has someplace in particular to go—as with a health spell for someone in another part of the country, when the magic is entering into an object—such as a charm or talisman, and when you are releasing energy into the Universe to affect a change—such as bringing wealth to you. Gestures figure into the work by pointing the way, by ushering the energy to a general direction for action, or for directing the energy into the spell item. Set up your materials for the spell so that by the time you are ready to energize the magical item it is on top of a pentacle (the disk with an encircled pentagram on it representing Earth—for manifestation), which may be made of wood, tile, ceramic, or even paper. Your hands, in a sweeping motion or in a gesture using a single emphatic shake, will point the way for the energy, and help a spell to flow in a specific direction. If, as an example, you want your magic to go to New York City, and you live in Illinois, as you end the spell direct it with your hands motioning to the east.

The next phase is to actually send the raised energy to accomplish the task. During the spell work, you have, as an example, inscribed a candle, lit it, dropped herbs into the flame while stating the intent, then chanted and motioned to raise energy, gathered the energy together and pointed it into the candle spell, spoken the focus word, and directed the energy with hands or wand in the direction the spell should travel, and *now* you need to release it. This is accomplished by envisioning the energy as instantly departing, with nothing lingering behind. It is very important to not leave out this step. You are winding up the energy, concentrating it to a task, telling it where to go, so *send* it. Once that is done, take a cleansing breath—inhale deeply and exhale—and see the energy as departed. You should sense an *emptiness* in the space where the magic was performed, unless you have installed the energy within an object, in which case, you should sense the energy as separate from you and residing within the object, vibrating on its own. See the spell as successfully completed, ground the residual energy with a blessing to the Earth for helping you in your work, and have some refreshment.

Twin Aspects of Magical Work: Purpose and Method

Identifying the Purpose

When it comes to creating your spell, you need to identify the purpose, which is not as easy as it sounds. Sometimes there is confusion between the desired outcome (or goal) and the purpose, but if you delineate to yourself what it is that you want to accomplish, and feel it, then your work will be directed to the purpose of the spell. Suppose, for example, that you merely like someone, but that person appears to be very dependent upon you. You want independence, but don't want to hurt anyone's feelings. Doing a spell to find a compatible partner for your friend would be a goal that would accomplish the purpose, namely of relieving you of feeling responsible for this person. But the partner is really not the problem, so you would need to address the real issue: that you do feel responsible, not that you need to be doing spells involving relationships for

people who have not asked for them. The true *purpose* of the spell, then, is to release *yourself* from the burden of unwanted emotional ties to this person. That makes the spell for you and addresses your feelings about the situation.

Now that the purpose of the spell is known, you can focus on achieving the desired outcome, letting go. Use your list of correspondences to construct the spell according to the associations of the topics (herbs, colors, days, hours, etc.).

Have a single word/image in mind to state when energy is raised so you can send it out at the end of the spell—perhaps something like "freedom." Raise the energy with any of the previously discussed methods, direct the energy into the spell with the keyword, and release it to accomplish the task.

But how to get started? Before you begin planning any spell, you need to focus inward and decide what it is you are attempting, and why. Here is when you apply the ethics of the Craft to your work, knowing that there is balance in the flow of energy, and understanding that you do not have the moral right to direct magic at or for another person without that person requesting it. In my *Green Witchcraft* books I talk about the Rules of Conduct that were taught to me by my mother, who told me her mother did the same with her. She recited this code of Craft Ethics to me throughout my childhood and early adolescence, and this is what I use in my practice. There are other ethical codes as well, with the most familiar in modern Wicca being the one popularized by Gerald Gardner as the Witches' Rede. The core ethical value from the lengthy Rede resides in the words stating that a practitioner may do whatever is desired, whatever is willed, so long as it harms none. This is reinforced with the warning that any magical energy sent out by the practitioner will return to the sender threefold. There are some versions of the Rede that make allowances for sending negative energies by inserting a statement of exception, indicating that the rule of three is held in abeyance when magic is worked in personal self-defense. Nevertheless, the primary moral admonition of the Rede is that you harm none, which includes yourself. While not all Traditions are in agreement about the inclusion of an exemption for acting in self-defense since it appears to offer an inferred allowance to do harm, it does conform with the ceremonial magician concept of a threefold return for those who fail in their magical workings, so ceremonial background could be a factor here.

For some people, even self-defense is not an excuse to work magic against another. I agree with this because I feel that there are many ways to respond in self-defense without creating a direct magical action, and some of those options will be covered in this chapter.

The Rules of Conduct as I learned them and have written about them has the basic warning that the energy you send out, whether in magical work or demeanor, will draw like energy to you, so you have to make informed decisions and be conscious of the implications of your energies. If you are filled with negativity, you will draw more to you, so you need to address your own needs before attempting magic for anyone else. Much of the magical work is intended for self-improvement, so your own energy needs to be bright and orderly before you can begin to think about magic for others. The ethical standard of Green Witchcraft lies in the following Rules of Conduct:

> *Be careful what you do.*
> *Be careful who you trust.*
> *Do not use the Power to hurt another because what is sent*
>   *comes back.*
> *Never use the Power against someone who has the Power,*
>   *for you both draw from the same well.*
> *To use the Power, you must feel it in your heart and know it*
>   *in your mind.*

The first rule warns you to think through the details of any spell or magical working rather than leaping into action. You have to look at the situation objectively and ensure that your magic will perform as intended without stifling another person's freedom and individuality. Even when you feel you can help someone, you need that person's consent, lest you interfere with their karmic challenges for this lifetime. There are exceptions, of course, such as in protecting a loved one from injury, but only you know what your relationship is with this person. If it is a matter of life or death, and the person is not available for comment, it becomes a personal judgment call, as it was when my mother and I did candle magics to protect my brother when she felt he was in danger. He was, and could have died leaving the field of battle after his tour of duty in Vietnam, but instead moved without injury through a sequence of three life-threatening events (he stepped on a land mine that failed to explode, the evacuation helicopter he was in was shot down, the second one he entered was also shot down, and finally he departed successfully on the third one). My brother lived another thirty years with his wife, bringing three beautiful daughters into the world. So while it is natural to try to assist someone in need, unless you have tacit approval and are dealing with close kin, for optimal effectiveness, a person should request or at least consent to your aid.

The rule of "Be careful who you trust" may have come down from the persecutions of midwives, herbalists, and others who held to the Old Ways in the past, and so keeping quiet about magical practices was a necessity for survival. Today the issue of being public about your beliefs and spiritual path is still determined by how much opposition or harassment you anticipate and are willing to endure from your neighbors and associates. It is difficult to determine at face value whether the people who claim to be open-minded would continue to be so in the face of a practicing Wiccan in their midst. These same people may be accepting or may be actually quite conservative or narrow-minded where spirituality and magic are concerned. Your need to judge wisely, based upon your own circumstances, makes this rule pertinent, even today.

"Do not use the power to hurt another because what is sent comes back" means that the energies you invoke will eventually travel full circle, and so you want to move energy, whether light or shadow, in a positive manner. It may be that you need to examine your motives and find an alternate way of dealing with the problems that come up in daily life. Magic should never be used frivolously for revenge over some issue. The energy released will draw like energy back to you. This is something that my mother was always concerned about, and she would tell us not to talk about "bad things" because this attracted them. I have noticed over the years that the people who complain the most usually draw the most negative energy to themselves, so I can see that her words make sense. The energy you send creates reactions and ripples in the energy field of the Earth, eventually bringing the flow back to you. The greater the power you expend when you initiate a magical action, the faster the return.

The caution against using the Power against someone who has the Power means that there is kinship among magic workers. I always cringe when I hear people talk about "Witch wars" and I prefer to neutralize the verbal expression so that mentally, the image is of bickering people struggling with personality conflicts and egotism rather than one of bloody warfare. High-octane words should be used with care, especially among those who move energy and practice visualizing thought into manifestation. In Celtic tradition, the ties of kinship are based upon that of blood, but for the Witch, the ties of kinship are of spirit. We of the Craft are related through energy as brothers and sisters, and as such, no matter how we interact on a personal basis, we are still kin to one another and deserve to be treated with respect. This does not mean you have to associate with people you disagree with, merely that it is not appropriate to demand that others follow your particular path. Witchcraft is not about "the one true way," and Witches recognize that there are many paths to the Divine. Kinfolk should never harm one another, and you must respect other practitioners of the Craft as you respect the Craft itself. Most Initiations include this admonition against bringing harm to any others of the Craft with the reminder that the initiate is joining with others in a spiritual relationship to the Lady and the Lord.

The last rule speaks to the internal working of magical energy. This means that magic is not a matter of faith but of knowing—it is kenned. When you ken something, you feel it is so without any doubt or notions to the contrary. The movement of magical energy is like that, and so to work successful magic, there is no room for doubt. You have to accept, both mentally and intuitively, that your magic will produce results, and the sensation is actually very casual, often considered a type of altered state or alpha state. Once you have experienced this sensation, you will always recognize it.

A code of ethics is important to follow, not only to avoid harming others, but to avoid harming yourself. When you are manipulating energy, you are still part of the cycle of life and part of the energy flow. By harming another, you bring harm to yourself, because like energy attracts like energy. This extends even to the realm of thought. When you continually think negatively, that is the energy you draw to yourself so that your thoughts become a self-fulfilling prophecy. By thinking positively, that type of energy will be drawn to you, so the state of mind is very important in the conducting of magic. Magic, just like an idea, begins in the mind. Here is where the groundwork is laid for the energy flow you are trying to create, and this is why you must operate from an ethical and moral foundation. To do otherwise will result in misdirected energy, ineffective magical work, nervousness, illness, and even paranoia. Magic is not a game, and to conduct magic, you must accept that it is real, and that it therefore carries consequences. Adopting a working ethic and abiding by it is the first major step toward a successful magical practice.

Type of Spell Defined by Purpose

In determining what the purpose of your magical work is, you must keep the ethical aspect in mind. Spells can be created for a variety of outcomes, but all of these can be whittled down into three basic types of purpose: *drawing, repelling,* and *containment.* These purposes can be illustrated with key words. Drawing spells are intended to *bring* something to you, while repelling spells *cast away* from you something already present, and containment spells *shield* you from something external, while simultaneously providing you with a secure interior. Containment works in two directions, then, so that by shielding the inner space from the entrance of undesired energy, you are effectively holding desired energy within an area, which affords you with a protected space. Some people may consider protection to be a fourth type of purpose, but I feel that a retaining purpose is part of containment, and protection is a product derived from containment. With protection, you are either *drawing* protective energies or you are keeping these existing or previously drawn energies around yourself while you *shield* yourself from exterior energies. These purposes may be utilized in both light and dark power magic by slightly altering the approach to energy movement.

Drawing spells are among the most commonly used of the magical purposes, for you are bringing something to yourself. Money spells, love spells, health spells performed as a reaction to illness, employment-seeking spells, and bringing protection to you or your home spells are all examples of drawing spells. Your purpose is to fill a need, or to bring something positive into your life. The attraction power is enhanced with timing, appropriate herbs, symbols, colors, and the wording you use in the creation of your spell. Your focus is identified and stated, and the raised energy is used to pull the necessary positive energies to you to reach your goal.

Repelling spells are used to cast away from you those existing things in your life that are unwanted. This process includes the categories of banishing and exorcising in that the spells address energies that are present and are being directed away, with the intent of clearing away the negative in order to make room for positive energies to enter. Here is where your creativity comes into play to make your Craft an art, for your needs are not always consistent with the obvious Moon phase. By adjusting your focus, your perspective, to fit the situation, you are able to manipulate energy to accomplish your goal. Let us say that you need money, but the Moon is in the waning phase of decrease represented by the Crone. You could wait until the Moon enters into the waxing phase of increase or you could redefine the parameters of your spell to fit the Waning Moon. By thinking in terms of banishing poverty, the opposite effect is naturally generated, thus to lose poverty or want, you necessarily gain money or increase of income. You then word your spell to take away the lack of money or the need for greater income. The spell materials will be those that address gain rather than loss, and thus reinforce the true intent. On the other hand, feeling an oppressive sense of depression and negative energy around you can be countered by a spell that exorcises those energies. This process will create an opening for you to follow up on with a spell that attracts or draws in positive energies. Magic used to repel energies is also part of home protection in which you may place salt over the entry doorways or a garlic clove in the corner of these doorways. A simple ritual such as sweeping the sacred space prior to casting a circle involves this type of magic purpose, for chaotic, negative energies are being swept away.

There is a fine line here between repelling and containment magics, with containing spells having a variety of uses as well. In the above example, after the repelling purpose of sweeping the circle, the containment purpose is used to fill the circle with light and love, as well as to hold the energy that is subsequently raised until it is released. Containment spells are also the ones you weave to keep desired energies in your home, such as through the sprinkling of herbs around rooms, burning incense, or lighting a candle at a home shrine or altar. At the same time, another type of containment involves providing a place for negative energies to be gathered for later disposal, and so you might hang a braid of garlic or onion in the kitchen for this absorption task. The hanging of the braid may be part of a Samhain or Hogmanay (New Year's Eve) celebration during which last year's braid is removed and the new year's braid is installed. I like to use a garlic braid, but my mother preferred an onion braid for indoor containment, and additionally tucked garlic cloves in the doorway to repel negativity.

When you cleanse a house by going through each room with candlelight, incense, and consecrated water, invoking the blessings of the Divine, you are containing positive energies in your home. If you perform this ritual in conjunction with gathering negative energies to the candlelight, then escorting them out the back door, you are combining purposes with collecting undesired energies to the candle in order to be repelled out of doors, while also containing the purified atmosphere of Divine blessing within the house. Combining purposes is another factor in spell crafting, which you may do as long as you are clear in your own mind as to the sequence of events. Otherwise, you may prefer to do the drawing and repelling spell in the above example, then go back through the house and do a house blessing in which the invoked energies are contained within.

Besides keeping things closed in, containment spells may utilize attributes of *deflection* and *reflection*. The containment focus, however, may be close to you or far from you, depending upon the need and circumstance. With the house blessing, you are containing the desired energy fields within your home, but containment may also be applied as passive defense magic, with this latter being most often associated with negative energies that are directed toward you. Using containment, deflection, and reflection as a self-defense purpose allows you to magically respond to threats to your peace and your energy field without acting contrary to the ethics of the Wiccan Rede or Rules of Conduct.

Dark power/negative energy may be directly accessed and manipulated through the use of repelling or containment spells, which turn the generated negative energies back to their source. This is not the creation of new energy, merely the distracting or bending of existing energy, rather like catching a baseball and throwing it back to the pitcher. Done properly, the energy is simply gathered, spun around, then released.

In a case where you feel that there is negative energy being deliberately directed toward you for whatever reason, you can respond with a containment spell that activates as deflection or reflection. With containment alone, you are restricting the negative energy to the auric field of the sender prior to it being launched. The result of this is that the energy being generated by someone (perhaps through anger, envy, or some other such motivation) will be unable to escape the sending person's own energy field. The inherent meaning to this is that the sending individual will become neutralized by feeling the brunt of his or her own energies. This type of spell work may be used as a follow-up to a deflection or reflection spell if the negative energy has already been projected toward you. Thus you would first deal with the negative energy, then use a containment spell to prevent further negative energy from being propelled at you.

Deflection spells dissipate negative energies directed toward you by scattering the energies in a myriad of directions so that, through diffusion, the power is so weakened it is rendered harmless, no matter where it eventually alights. A common example of such a spell is that of the witch's bottle. This is a glass jar that typically contains broken glass, mirror shards, pins, nails, thorns, and other sharp objects, and sometimes urine. The jar is buried on the edge of the property or by the front door. In America's Colonial days this practice was quite prevalent (including the addition of urine), and it seems to be undergoing a revival. The spell becomes active once the bottle is buried, and the deflection purpose is invoked during the spell crafting to energize the bottle.

Reflection spells are also protective, with the negative energies that have already been directed to you doing an about-face and affecting the original sender. This is called a *return-to-sender* spell where the energies are neither disbursed randomly nor prevented from escaping a person's auric field, but turned around to ricochet back to the sender so that it is the sender who receives the force of his/her own negative energy before it dissipates. This is the type of spell that may utilize a mirror that has been magically charged and placed to face the direction of the incoming energy (do not look into the mirror after it has been charged). It is typical to use these mirrors buried facing outward at the four corners of your habitation or at the quarters along the perimeter of your yard for protection of home and property. But in the case of a sudden need, when you feel someone is directing negative energies at you (yes, this does happen), a simple cosmetic mirror may be quickly charged to briefly reflect negative energies and held circumspectly toward the source of that energy. Once the task has been completed, the compact mirror is released from this duty by telling it, or by blowing on it, or by passing it through heat and smoke, so that it reverts to being a make-up tool.

Your own energies infuse everything around you, and when you are in the habit of practicing magic, the connections are open, providing you with access to the energy that turns mundane items into magical tools, if only for a few moments. My grandmother used cigarette smoke for any number of protective devices. While smoking was an inconspicuous action, she could avail herself of the inherent power of tobacco, and blow the smoke in a quick puff to the object she magically enhanced or cleansed. She used breath work in her magics, but she was also a wondrous healer through herbs and the Power. To both her and my mother, tobacco, black tea (liquid or leaf), and coffee (liquid or grounds) were seen as energizers to spell work. I still like to use black tea, and I will use incense smoke, but tobacco is used only in leafy form, making an excellent additive to offerings to the Earth Mother or included in a magical amulet or mojo bag. Through using a mirror in reflection magic, you bounce the negative energies back to the point of origin, without obstructing the flow of positive energies.

In all that you do, you must keep in mind the ethics of not causing harm to another. These techniques do not involve initiating negative magic toward a person, but act upon the existing energy already initiated by another to return it back to the original sender, who is responsible for his/her actions. Deflection magic has the most passive purpose in that it diffuses and scatters negative energies, rendering them harmless. Containment magic is the least passive in that it restricts the negative energy to remain within its sphere of origin. I envision the containment of this sort of energy as similar to placing a clear bowl over the perpetrator. The energy continues to bounce off the ceiling and back to the person like steam in a pressure cooker until the person either stops generating and lets things cool down, or becomes worn out from the effort of maintaining the negative sendings, which also has the effect of making the sender stop generating the negative energy.

With containment magic, the individual issuing the negative energy will feel a growing unease, then an energy drain will leave the person worn out, which has the effect of turning off the heat so that personal recuperation can begin. But if the individual is persistent, refusing to let go of the directed rage or malice, the energy drain will take the natural course, leading again to exhaustion so that the person can no longer sustain the negative energy. The difference between people and pressure cookers is the connection to the Earth—the energy has only one escape route, through the sender and into the ground. Here, Nature can convert and/or redirect the energy where needed, which is why the containment should be viewed as placing a bowl over the sender rather than encapsulating the person.

There is a general misunderstanding about negative energy that needs to be considered—not all negative or dark energy is undesirable. This is the type of energy that drives chaos, from which we get those sudden bursts of inspiration, ideas, and creativity, breathing new life into what would otherwise turn stagnant. Without chaos, order becomes unappealing due to the lack of constructive and creative vitality. The unrealistic view of dark energy relating to evil while light energy relates to good is the product of social and cultural programming. The *qualities* are not the same as the *energies*, and to equate them amounts to a comparison of totally different things. Dark and light energies exist in balance, as may be illustrated by the image of Yin and Yang, with a little of each in the other, and by the polarity of magnetic energy fields. Sometimes those polarities switch, just as the Earth's polarity does, although on a grander time scale. My point is that dark or negative energy is not necessarily *bad* and light or positive energy is not always *good*—these are qualities assigned by societal and cultural associations. It is up to you to decide what works best for you, what gives you peace and balance without stifling your individuality and sense of aliveness.

Type of Spell Defined by Method

The second aspect of magic is the method. There are various types of magical methods, and your spell work will be more effective if you understand how you will attain what you are trying to accomplish. While the **purpose** was the *reason* for the magic, the **method** is the *how* of the magic—this is how you approach your spell crafting. I have a different perspective on the methods of Witchcraft than what is normally found in other sources, especially those derived from ceremonial magic. In order to see the difference, we need to first look at what are some commonly accepted terms relating to methods of spell work.

I have read and heard people talk about Witchcraft using *sympathetic* magic, with the word "primitive" occasionally used to further describe it. I feel that the term "sympathetic" has undergone a change over the past few decades, so that it has come to be used frequently as implying that since all things are connected through energy, ALL magic is sympathetic, since it is performed through some kind of correlation.

I have also come across the term "contagion" as an aspect of sympathetic magic utilizing something that has been in contact with the subject of the magical working. Here is where a piece of clothing or snip of hair is brought into the spell to enhance the focus, as with a health spell (as the examples I have seen usually give as their examples). But the reality is that this is where you are more likely to be approached by someone offering snips of hair and scraps of clothing with the hope that you will do a spell affecting an unsuspecting third party who originally possessed the item—which is a serious breach of ethics! Needless to say, this is not a good practice, so unless the items belong to the person offering them for spell work, they are best declined. Health spells, incidentally, can be quite effectively done without such items, but these things are very useful in protection spells.

Another term I have seen relating to magic is "homeopathic," which simply means the use of correlations (drawn from your lists of correspondences in your BOS) in sympathetic magic, such as lighting a green candle during a money spell.

But since sympathetic magic is described as being performed through some kind of correlation, the terms contagion and homeopathic merely differentiate the type of correlation. The first, then, is something that has been in contact with the subject, and the second is something that has not, but is instead drawn from your list of correspondences. Since contagion and homeopathic are subcategories, once again, the *only* type of magic that is viewed is *sympathetic* magic, or so the common acceptance indicates.

But none of this is how I learned it in my family heritage. What I will cover now are the methods of conducting magic that I was taught, but remember at all times that these methods are used in tandem with the ethics learned from the Rules of Conduct. While magic is conducted for a variety of reasons, the inherent responsibility on the part of the practitioner through a code of ethics is imperative, lest the results generate a serious psychic and spiritual endangerment of your spiritual Self (Mannuz). The admonition of "Harm none" refers to the magic worker as well as the object of the magical energy. I was taught that there are four magical methods for conducting spells: **sympathetic, comparative, directive,** and **transference,** and I was taught the difference between them through key phrases, which I consider important enough to indicate here in bold print quotes.

Sympathetic Magic

Sympathetic magic means: **"This IS that."** In other words, an object that is unrelated to the subject of the spell is visualized, seen, and treated, as *being* that subject. This means that whatever happens to the magical object, happens to the subject. The example that comes quickly to mind is the use of poppets, or voodoo dolls, but sympathetic magic may involve any number of objects that are then seen as being the subject of the spell. In my classes I use the example of a lost dog being led home through moving a toy dog closer to a dollhouse over a period of hours or days, for example. This method may include something belonging to the object of the spell—such as a doggy toy, but this type of magic was most certainly used in the older style love/attraction spells in which a piece of paper or cloth is pronounced as, "this is (name X) . . ." then as the item is burned in a candle flame, ". . . burning with love for me." This latter example is most likely to be what people have in mind when you are approached with those snips of hair and scraps of cloth I mentioned earlier, and you are asked to do a spell—and this is when you have to put your ethical foot down.

The idea behind sympathetic magic is that the spell object becomes the actual subject of the spell, thus you could bring the lost dog home because the actual dog must follow the path of the toy dog to the house. Here you are saying that as things affect the ritual object, so is the subject of the spell affected. Thus, if you are worried that your lost dog is hungry or thirsty, you may offer a drink and bite of food to the toy, and *know* that your dog will also find food and drink on the way home.

The sympathetic method may also include those candle burning spells in which items are burned in the flame or the candle is inscribed using symbols (a dollar sign, as an example), sigils and seals which **are** the object of the spell. You construct the wording of the spell appropriately, such as inscribing the candle near the rim so that as the symbol is melted, the magic is released. A sigil may be constructed from an alphabet arranged in segments in a circle. Choose a key word for your spell, then using the circle of letters, draw a continuous line to each letter of the word, starting the line with a circle and ending it with a capping line (like a "T"). The shape that results is your sigil, which you copy onto the candle. The example of the Witch's Sigil Wheel on page 57 of *Green Witchcraft III* is a common circular shape, but any shape can be used for developing your sigil—you could arrange the letters of the alphabet in a square, rectangle, or triangle and draw your sigil from that as well. Seals, however, are magical diagrams using the numerical equivalent of a person's or spirit's name and placing it within the numerical square of a planet, with a resulting design that can then be placed under the spell object when the spell is conducted during the day and the hour of the planetary influence involved. Seals are characteristic of ceremonial magic, but sigils and bindrunes, which are monograms of two to three runic letters invoking their combined magical meanings, are typical in Witchcraft. This will be further explored in the next chapter.

One of the ancient uses of sympathetic magic was in the search for game and a successful hunt. Prehistoric cave art in several European sites show hunting scenes in a sequence that infers the hunt was performed in ritual prior to the actual pursuit of game. Another ancient example of how sympathetic magic was traditionally used is to encourage fertility. There are numerous images of pregnant women, indicating both the sense of a Mother Goddess, and an invocation of fertility through these images. The use even today of standing stones and holed stones as fertility symbols in which a woman sits upon one or passes through the other to become pregnant shows the continuing tradition of fertility-oriented sympathetic magic.

Another use of sympathetic magic is in protection spells, often using a root such as that of bronze fennel, in which the object is dressed as or viewed as a particular person and placed in a protective environment (particularly if the person is in a dangerous place such as a battlefield). Promotion and well-being may be part of this type of magic as well. The reverencing of images of the Goddess and the God may invoke sympathetic magic if you see the image as being the Divine and hence accessible. In Roman Catholicism, sympathetic magic is used when a statue of a saint is turned to face the wall until something desired occurs, but the saint used is one whose energies relate to specific desires or to a locale. If a church is dedicated to Saint Anthony, the clergy could see the saint's statue as influential in any church or clergy matter. If a lay member wants to sell his or her home, a statue of St. Joseph might be buried until the deal is accomplished. The action taken toward the image is seen as affecting the deity or saint depicted. With Santeria, images are fed or nourished with rum, while with Witchcraft, offerings are made before the images of the Lady and the Lord at altars or shrines. The consecration of a statue ritual (page 145–153, *Green Witchcraft III*) employs sympathetic magic in the drawing down of the energy of the Divine into the statue so as to enliven the image and maintain a sacred presence therein.

Comparative Magic

Comparative magic means: ***"This REPRESENTS that."*** This is one of the most familiar methods to practitioners of Witchcraft. With this type of representational spell, you establish a relationship between two objects, drawing a connection between the objects used in the spell or charm and the focus of the spell or charm. This is most commonly seen in charms and growth spells. An example of a charm is the creating of an Elemental Bottle to enhance your connection between the Elementals and yourself, while an example of a growth spell is the planting of a seed and saying that as the plant grows, so does . . . (wealth, friendships, success, etc.). Because of their great versatility, candles may be burned with this approach as well, with the wording of the spell or the additives to the candle aiding in the focus. One such spell would be to have "money to burn" by burning a dollar bill in the candle flame.

The difference between this representational method and the sympathetic method is that with comparative magic you do not have to erase the mental line between the spell item and the object of the spell. You can continue to see these two as separate, but know (ken) that one item is able to affect the other through the energy raised and sent. If you have a well-developed imagination, sympathetic magic may come easier, but if you are more prone to analysis, comparative magic may prove a better method. The main thrust of the spell work is to draw a relationship between the actions of the materials used and the actions of the spell object.

With the Elemental Bottle, you place in the jar objects that represent the Elementals, while the fired pottery container represents you, thus displaying the relationship between yourself and the Elementals—they are part of you (clay, water, kiln, and necessary action of air to make the pot relate it to your body with flesh, fluids, cellular energy, and breath) and reside within you (your connection to them makes the Elementals your close kin). Now you have an altar object that brings a visual tie between yourself and the Elementals upon whom you call at circle casting and during spell work.

The main way to identify comparative magic is with the word "as" being used, or through a demonstration of the relationship between the spell item and the object of the spell: "As this incense burns, so is this house cleansed." The major factor is your focus, and so you have to know what you are trying to achieve, and move the energies raised to that purpose. Charms are often made with comparative magic, with the ingredients or designs inscribed being addressed with the purpose while being constructed: "As this ginger root represents success, and the sigil inscribed upon it represents career gains, these are drawn to me at work when I carry this mojo bag in my briefcase." Whenever you conclude a spell with the tradition words, "As I will, So Mote It Be!" you are emphasizing the comparative magic of the spell or sealing the spell with comparative magic energy, normally drawn up from the Earth for manifesting power. This action is sometimes so subtle you are barely aware of the source of that sealing energy.

Directive Magic

Directive magic means: *"**This AFFECTS that.**"* This is perhaps the most common method when using herbs and stones in Witchcraft. It involves the raising of energy, focusing it on a goal, directing the energy, and releasing it to accomplish the goal. Most candle-burning magics are directive in nature, especially when herbs, stones, or crystals are added to the flame. When herbs are dropped into a candle during spell work, you are directing the energy of the plant to the purpose, or direction, of the spell. You may simply state, "bergamot for wealth," as you add the herb to the spell, but the energy flow means that the bergamot affects your prosperity.

Energy is moved in a directive form when you raise it and send it to a particular place. Magic created for drawing money, finding a job, enhancing health, and so forth may be enhanced by the energy of chanting, dancing, altered breathing, or drumming, which is then focused with a word form (for a money spell, the spoken word could be "wealth!"), then directed in a flowing motion of your hands or wand into the spell object (such as a green candle). It is next released for accomplishment with another motion that sends the gathered energy away from the spell object to perform its task. This is why you normally bury or dispose of spell materials after use— they are depleted of energy and form an energy vacuum. Unless recharged periodically by raising and directing more energy (usually Earth energy) into a spell object, you risk having the vacuum filled with undesired energies. Burying the object in the ground allows the Earth to take the depleted spell material and decompose it. Similarly, one reason you toss out offerings after they have sat on the altar or shrine is that the *essence* has been consumed—the energy is gone. You never eat offerings because there is no flavor left, the texture is cardboardy or sandy, and there is an energy void in the material which would be filled by your own vital energies. Another variety of spell casting requires burial of the spell materials for dissemination through the Earth. The basic concept, however, is that the energy raised in one place during a spell is being directed—moved—to another place, either to bring something to you or to affect something in that other place.

Transference Magic

Transference magic means: *"This ENTERS that."* This type of spell has various degrees of intensity, with the highest levels only used with extreme caution and dire need. Transference magic in a spell moves a clearly detrimental energy out of one place or person and into something else, with the absolute awareness that this absorption will be harmful to the recipient. Because the code of ethics admonishes us not to harm another, this spell in the high intensity level may only be worked under extreme circumstances and only with the consent of the recipient of the negative energy, which generally weakens and/or dies.

At its mildest form, transference magic is typical in protection spells, such as those in which you hang a garlic or onion braid in your kitchen to absorb negative energies. You do not use the cloves or bulbs in your cooking, but keep it instead as a Craft decoration whose magical purpose is to draw and hold onto undesired energies. Even with this simple magical item, you must bless the braid and respect the gift of self-sacrifice on the part of the garlic, consecrating it by passing it through the symbols of the Elementals. When you eat food or cook with food plants, their energy passes into you and becomes part of you, thus they continue to live. But with transference magic, you are interrupting this process so that the passage of energy into living tissue is denied the garlic or onion in the braid. With garlic, the interior will shrivel invisibly beneath the outer skin, so that while it may look the same after a year, if you touch the bulbs, you will find that they have become like a balloon with a tissue-thin covering. This ability to give of itself is one of the reasons garlic has such a high energy vibration and power for spell work. At the end of the year, dispose of the braid with a blessing for the sacrifice the plant made.

While the garlic braid may be considered a weaker intensity of transference magic, a stronger intensity is typically illustrated by conducting a spell that moves the energy of an illness out of a person and into something else, usually a plant. Perhaps this is where the tradition of sending flowers to hospital patients developed. Not only do plants, especially cut flowers, cheer up a person with their energies, they absorb the negative energies surrounding the recipient and eventually die. With a magical application, as the plant withers, the person heals. An even stronger intensity ordinarily exists between mothers and their children. This is demonstrated with the transference of energy affected by a mother taking on to herself the debilitation of her child because she may feel she is stronger and more capable of coping with it. The result can be that the mother is able to dissipate those negative energies, or that as the child grows healthy, the mother becomes ill, then uses her own energy reserves to drive the illness away. Love for the child is what activates the energy transference. But the most powerful intensity is that in which one life ends that another life may continue. This may occur when deleterious energies are voluntarily taken on by a loving pet or a familiar in a act of devotion, protection, and spiritual self-improvement. A transference spell of this sort moves the adverse energies from the family member into the pet, which under some conditions may actually be better equipped than the person to handle this energy, or the pet may succumb to the adverse energy. But this method of magic is an ethical minefield that must be trod with the greatest of care.

With all magic, retention of a code of ethics or the Rules of Conduct of the Green Craft is necessary, particularly: "Be careful what you do" and "Do not use the power to hurt another because what is sent comes back." All the entities of the Earth are alive with the spirit of the Divine and are your kin. These entities, including plants and animals, are able to communicate to the Witch whether or not they are willing to help. Part of being a Witch is being able to sense and communicate with plants and animals; how else would you know what leaf an herb is offering to you for your spell work? Actually, these living things usually suggest the transfer of energy, offering themselves as willing containers from love, devotion, generosity, or as a means of cleansing their own personal auras and so improving themselves spiritually. This is a priceless gift, and if accepted must be done with utmost reverence, respect, and love.

If you attempt transference magic without the consent of the recipient you will suffer severe physical, psychic, and spiritual repercussions. You will essentially end up drawing the transferred energy directly into yourself, but the route it takes could add to the negativity, especially if the unsolicited recipient dies. In this case, besides bringing the original energy into yourself, you will attract the spirit of the recipient in hostility, thus doubling the negative effect. Because you violated the ethics, your own auric field would be diminished, making the return of the energy three times as powerful. Indeed, this is the only time in the Green Craft where the idea that what is sent comes back threefold is found. If the recipient forgives you, the return is two-fold rather than three-fold. The overall effect of working without consent will most likely be failure in your efforts to heal or protect a loved one, and self-injury to a degree dependent upon the amount of returning energy, such as when augmented by those of the intended recipient and your own weakened auric field.

My mother used to tell me that negative energy may be transferred unconsciously by other people through envy, or it may occur as an inherent, place-centered negative atmosphere that then seeps into a vulnerable person who enters the area. This is one reason for doing a house cleansing prior to moving in or soon afterwards—you want to neutralize and purge any leftover energies from previous dwellers so that the house is refreshed and ready to have its atmosphere aligned with your personal energies. Children, the elderly, and the infirm are the most susceptible to negative energy that has stayed within a dwelling, so censing the house and invoking positive energies has many benefits. A cleansing, whose purpose then is to repel or exorcise the energy, may be constructed using the directive method, with the garlic braid being the height of the transference aspect of the spell.

Putting Purpose and Method Together

In a quick review of the moving of magical energy, there are three types of purpose: Drawing; Repelling (including banishing/exorcising); and Containment (including deflecting/reflecting). And there are four types of method: Sympathetic (*"this IS that"*); Comparative (*"this REPRESENTS that"*); Directive (*"this AFFECTS that"*); and Transference (*"this ENTERS that"*).

You decide what your purpose is for spell work, so that once this is known, you can plan on how to achieve the desired outcome. Use your list of correspondences to construct the spell according to the correlations of the topics (herbs, colors, days, hours, etc.), and according to the structure of the spell (charm, candle burning, sachet, poppet, potpourri, knot tying, etc.). You may want to have a single word/image in mind to state when energy is raised so you state this as you send the energy out at the end of the spell.

As an example, let us say that you are moving into a new home and want to cleanse it of any lingering negativity from the past dwellers. Besides *repelling* (or *exorcising*) any existing negative energies for a cleansing, you may want to go beyond that, to include the *containment* of the purified atmosphere along with the *deflection* of any returning negative energies. And lastly, you may choose to conclude your ritual by *drawing* positive energies into your cleansed home.

Having decided the threefold purpose of your magic and the important sequence of steps, you need to determine the methods for each step. Sympathetic magic would probably not be on the top of your list of choices, simply because it tends to imply distance. Unless you are cleansing your house in Buffalo while you are dwelling in your New York City studio apartment, sympathetic magic is not generally a house cleansing method. But since you have three functions in mind for the cleansing, the methods most likely to work are a combination of directive and transference magic. A smudge of sage incense may be carried through each room, perhaps along with a consecrated candle for the unwanted energies to be drawn to, then carried out of doors with the candle, and then released to the wind

91

when the candle is blown out. These two actions serve the purposes of repelling and drawing with a directive method ("this affects that"). A braid of garlic may now be hung up in the kitchen to absorb any future negativity, utilizing the containment (shielding) purpose through the transference method ("this enters that"). The third part of the ritual is to actually draw in positive energies, perhaps an invocation to the Divine while asperging the rooms with blessed water. The purpose here is drawing energy, while the method is directive in that you are invoking the desired energies. By additionally placing a Solar Cross over the door inside each room, your purpose would be containment of the positive energy drawn into the rooms, and your method would be comparative through the imagery of the Solar Cross and the Sacred Light of the Divine ("this represents that").

When you plan your magical work, by knowing your purpose and your method, you can look through your list of correspondences in your BOS and select the day, time, incense, candle color, and so forth for the construction of your cleansing spell. You may want to use the command, "Go!" when you release the unwanted energies outside, and you may want to use the word, "Peace!" as you asperge each room, or "Light!" when placing the Solar Crosses. When you are finished with the magical work, you must release the excess energy you have channeled by placing your palms on the floor, and then take some refreshment before bidding farewell to the Elementals and the Divine and putting away your tools.

Inner Magic

Getting in Touch with Energies

To begin almost any spell, you should plan ahead, making sure you have sufficient materials, and work during the most advantageous preparation time. You can indeed do "spells on the run," and I've done them myself, but there is a very satisfying sense of communion with the Divine when you take the time to think through the steps and then perform a full ritual. A need for major ritual spell work does not turn up everyday. Even so, I do not subscribe to the notion that you need to study for years before attempting spells, particularly since there are a surprising lot of little spells that are done which may not even be thought of as such. The extension of energy to hold the traffic light green until you are through the intersection, the envisioning of the empty parking space at the crowded shopping center, the movement between the beats of time to arrive at work without being late, the shielding of the car through heavy traffic to ward off accidents, the holding off of the downpour until indoors, and the finding of a desired item on the store shelf that wasn't there the first time you

looked—these are all little spells that the connected Witch tosses off during a normal day's routine, an opportunity to practice the Craft through living it. For the Witch, every aspect of the day is a magical moment, waiting to be dipped into or simply acknowledged with a smile or quickly raised eyebrow.

A Witch lives a magical life in which nothing is taken for granted. The rising and the setting of the Sun, the phases of the Moon, the movement of the planets and the constellations, the changing of the seasons, the shape, color, and movement of clouds, the taste of the air, the smell of the Earth and sky, the waving wildflowers, the hidden clumps of herbs, and the variety of creatures in our world all are experienced daily. Even the spirits of roadkill animals, possibly confused and alarmed, may be gently eased into the arms of the Lord of the Wildwood by your blessing. Even if already there, their spirits and your own will benefit from your blessing as you pass by.

Being aware of your surroundings and the energy flow around you is part of being alive and vitally involved with our world. It is so easy to become wrapped up in a routine that you forget to live the gift of life, that you stop seeing the world around you, fail to observe the drama of life in the trees, on the ground, in the air, and in the water. So if you find this has happened to you, make the time to sit in the park, to walk in the woods, or to pass through the garden. Awareness is not passive, but is a deliberate activity of opening your senses, your consciousness, and your subconsciousness to receive information. To manipulate energies you need to practice being alert to their presence, and noticing your environs is part of that practice, but you must do this with a sense of respect for these energies. These are part of the unity of energy from the Divine that we share on this planet, and as such, you are working with energies in a spirit of cooperation, not of dominance.

Talking to the plants, letting the trees know you appreciate the beauty of their turning leaves, greeting birds and butterflies, saying hello to the boulder you pass everyday, and speaking to the clouds are part of living the Craft—you are extending your awareness into your surroundings. Do not be surprised if things start to attract your attention that you never noticed before, because once you start regularly extending your awareness, the indwelling animal and plant spirits around you will respond. The Divine is in everything, so anything you talk to is listening, just as you listen. That is the second part of connection—listening.

The energy of devas and the Elementals are subtle and easily overlooked, so you need to deliberately reach out psychically to feel them as you commune with Nature. The spirits of other people are usually felt as a *presence*, and there will be times when that presence manifests in a form that varies according to your psychic ability to see the manifestation and the ability of the spirit to create the image.

There is an important difference between spirit and psychic energies. The first is the Divine essence of the being, while the second is the communicative and receptive powers of the being. Spirits are beings; psychic power is energy used by beings. Not all spirits are strong (possessed of great psychic energy), but they increase their strength either through helping others, as with being spirit guides or what are today called guardian angels, or through reincarnations in which they improve their spirit in the life they lead in material form. The strength of a spirit is described in terms of light, with a weak spirit being equated to the light of the sun at early dawn or late dusk, and a strong spirit being equated to the light of the sun at high noon. My mother and her mother were both very close to the spirits, and all three of us had experiences in which we were very aware of the presence and the assistance of spirits. For those who are interested in pursuing spirit communication, I recommend first asking the Divine for a strong spirit guide. Spirit communication can either take a lot of energy away from you or psychically overwhelm you with their previous life experiences if you are not grounded or if you are unassisted. Unless you are accustomed to working with plants and Nature, you may find it easier to feel spirit energies than those of the devas.

The movement of psychic energy is frequently experienced in daily matters so that it may go unnoticed. But it is through psychic energy that spell work and communion with the Divine are accomplished. These energies reveal themselves when you pick up sensations from other people, feeling an instant warmth or coldness, a like or dislike for someone, or an impression of an emotional state of being. This latter is generally transmitted through a person's aura, which may be sensed rather than noted visually, with anger being a prime example of this.

When you have questions and seek solutions to problems, you need to go beyond the asking of those questions and solutions— you need to pause and take a moment of inner quiet to listen for the answer. Psychic communication goes both ways—from you and to you. When you ask the Lady and the Lord to help you with some problem, give them a chance to respond before you rush off into another activity. The Divine will not ignore you, but you have to keep the communication channel open. One of the funniest examples I have seen of not keeping the channel open was televised in one of those periodic presentations meant to inform people about the activities of Witches. Of course the medium of television is tenuous at best for getting accurate information across, but in this case, the camera was focusing on a small group of Wiccans who were drawing down the Moon. Perhaps there was something edited, but the net result was that the part between drawing and releasing was missing. Instead, the camera caught the energy motions of the arms drawing in with, "Come down, oh Moon," then immediately reversing the motion of the arms with, "Blessed Be." I felt the yo-yo effect even as I watched. It was like the Moon was on a string of elastic!

When you feel there is a need for a more formal communication, there are meditations, the Esbats, and the Sabbat celebrations at their appropriate times. These can have little or great ritual, the choice is yours. There are also those moments of silence and stillness where you allow the Divine to give you guidance. But if you have a pressing need, and feel that spell work is the answer, then envision the spell as a magical communication in a different ritual context. When the spell is finished, you envision or see the result as in fact accomplished. Spirit energies may be very delicate, wispy and gossamer—particularly those of small plants and herbs such as marjoram and dill. Larger plants have stronger energies, and those with thorns tend to exert a wider aura than those without. Other spirit energies may come across as more substantial, and these are more likely to be the spirits of departed people or they may indicate the presence of the Elementals. My experience with the Elementals is that they are not *whats*, but *whoms*, and I know there are others who share this feeling.

Working with the Elementals

We call upon the Elementals during circle casting, for the cleansing and consecration of tools (see Appendix B for an example), and as part of the process of casting spells. They are invoked and farewelled, with blessings given and received, but who or what they are depends on the practitioner's point of view. To some, the Elementals may be little more than representations of the elements, but to others, they may be a presence, alive and intelligent, ready. For me, they are archetypes of the God and the Goddess expressed as individual entities and powers, and as such, they should never be summoned and dismissed as though they were personal servants. They are more than circle guardians who come and go, and they are more than the four elements of Earth, Air, Fire, and Water used in rituals. The acknowledgment of Elementals as emanations of the Divine and the inherent respect this generates may indicate that Green Witchcraft embraces certain aspects of the ancient *elementalism*. Since this is loosely defined as the worship of the elements as deities, the similarity is much more general in the Green Craft because the practice is not that of worship so much as that of oneness, connection, and therefore, communication.

The Elementals themselves may be described in terms of groupings of fours. While they are named as Earth, Air, Fire, and Water, the Elementals are also representative of the cardinal directions, primary colors (although which ones are assigned to which Elemental will vary with the Tradition), the four seasons, the four ages of human development, and aspects of the human psyche and body. With any of the Elemental associations, the Witch is able to more clearly focus the energy being moved through them into a magical working. Personal energy is added to spell work (enhanced by Earth energy drawn up during grounding and centering), and by recognizing the beingness of the Elementals you connect spiritually with them during the magic process. In the Green Craft they are called our *kith and kin*, meaning that they share in the same close-knit ties as family relations. The more you become accustomed to working with the Elementals, the more apparent their closeness to you becomes. They are dependable powers that you can address without a ritual or ceremony. You may use ritual to let them know your needs and wants, or you may simply think your desires or speak to them in a low whisper. They will respond, and when they do, you must be prepared to respect this and make use of their answer. The point here is that you do not ask something of the Elementals and when it appears, turn away from it. While the Elementals may have a sense of humor, they are not disposed to be petitioned, then rejected. They will be less responsive until you are able to mend the rift between you, and in the meantime, you are placing your own body in jeopardy. If you offend Water, you could start to retain body fluids, as an example, or if you offend Air, you might become short of breath or lose your creative edge. Always remember that courtesy is part of spell crafting, and integral to magical and personal relationships.

Together, the Elementals create a numerical four, emphasizing the manifesting aspect of your spell work with a number that describes a physical and solid foundation. Often the Elementals are grouped as two's where they afford a balance as pairs of dualities, unions, or opposites. Elementals Earth and Water may be considered as aligned with or as aspects of the Lady, while Elementals Air and Fire are aligned with or aspects of the Lord. Yet these alignments may be changed to fit your circumstance and envisioned relationship for your magical work, but in whatever correlation they are seen, the Elementals have and are Powers, and must be respected as such. Earth may represent the Goddess as harvest, bounty, barrenness, and upheaval. Water may represent the Goddess as love, nurturing, the life-giving waters, the sea, tempest, and storm. Thus the powers of the Goddess as Maiden, Mother, and Crone may be envisioned through the Elementals of Earth and Water. But the God may also be found in these two aspects as lord of the animals and protector of the wild places, as ruler of Underworld, and lord of the sea. How you perceive the Elementals, how you group them, and the correlations you make for them are all translated into your magical process. There are some examples of Elemental correlations in Appendix A under the listing of "Elemental Tides."

The power of the natural objects used in Green magics comes from your ability to focus on the desired Elemental correlation and funnel that energy through yourself and into your magical work. Everything that is used may be related in some manner to the Elementals: feathers (Air), rocks (Earth), shells (Water), pumice (Fire), and on it goes, with even Elemental aspects being applicable to what you might ordinarily think of as purely one aspect. With water, as an example, you can envision spring water (Water), storm water (Fire—for the lightning that has charged the water), rain water (Earth—for the ground absorption quality of a gently soaking rain), and mist or dew (Air—for the feathery lightness of the moisture). Likewise, various types of seeds and soil may be used in growth spells. Even when associating animal hair, fur, whiskers, claws [sheaths], and such with the characteristics of that animal (do not be alarmed by these examples as a house cat normally sheds all of the above, which may then be collected and used in spell work), the Elemental aspect is still drawn upon.

The Witchcraft rule of exchange is in effect here, meaning that in order to receive a gift, you must first give a gift. This exchange binds or connects the power and links the Elemental to the giver so that a gift may be released in turn. It is like an exchange of energy, and a unifying of energy, to accomplish a goal. The gift that you give may be an object such as a shiny penny, a symbol such as milk, or a blessing such as a pentagram drawn on the ground before a plant from which you need a leaf, but what matters is the sensation that accompanies the gift given and the kenning that prompts a return gift.

With each spell or ritual conducted in the Green Craft, the Elementals are contacted in some form. Whether the craftwork calls upon the energies of the light or the dark powers (as shown in *Green Witchcraft II*), the key to a successful Elemental alignment of aid is in your envisioning. For Earth, these elements are ground, trees, rocks, fields, forests, mountains, and four-legged animals like the bull, horse, and stag. For Air, there are wind, clouds, birds, butterflies, moths, and flying insects such as bees. For Fire, there are flame, molten magma, phosphorescence, lightning, lava, the salamander (traditionally believed to be able to live in fire), and the lion (associated with the desert, heat, and thus fire). Water may be envisioned as ocean, river, rain, spring, water table, pond, brook, fish (trout and salmon being associated since ancient times with wily wisdom), and sea mammals such as dolphins and whales (shelled sea creatures, such as crabs, lobsters, nautilus, and clams seem not to be used much, along with fleshy sea creatures such as the squid and octopus).

You are the one who determines what image of the Elemental you can relate to in your spell work. With a Full Moon-oriented circle and spell work, you might use images of a bull, eagle, salamander, and dolphin, whereas with a Dark Moon circle, you might use the images of a troll, will-o'-the-wisp, St. Elmo's fire, and a sea nymph (siren). For a Fairy magic circle, you could use the forms of a gnome or unicorn, sprite or Pegasus, dragon and mermaid, while for a dark power ritual, you could utilize forms that emphasize raw, untamed, highly energized power, such as an earthquake, tornado, volcanic eruption, and hurricane. Some people see different varieties of dragons at the Quarters, or simply shadowy, cowled figures. Whatever form is used depends on your receptiveness to that image. If trolls evoke for you the image of a rough, dusky, stony, earth-dwelling entity, then this will work for Elemental Earth. But if trolls remind you of a cute picture in a children's book or a little doll with long pink hair, this could prove a problem for focusing on Elemental Earth. By planning your work ahead, you are able to select the images that work for you and relate to the spell being cast, thus aiding in your focus of energy.

The main point to remember is that the Elementals are powers, and as such, should not be treated dismissively. Anyone who uses the word "only" to diminish their importance (". . . only working with Elemental energies . . .") apparently has never experienced an earthquake, tornado, volcanic eruption, hurricane, or flood. There are many people who, like myself, have experienced all of these demonstrations of Elemental power up close and personal: earth tremors in California, a tornado in Illinois, the eruption of Mount St. Helens in Washington, and Hurricane Andrew in Florida. There are plenty of other examples of devastating eruptions, floods, mudslides, and hurricanes, from Hawaii to Iceland, from the Mississippi and the Indus to the Yucatan Peninsula and the Andes Mountains, that should be sufficient to show that there is nothing insignificant about the Elementals. The movement of massive Elemental upheavals may be taken as a palpable example of the imbalance of our planet and the attempts by the Earth to reach an equilibrium. The more destructive we are of our environment, the more dark energy we throw into the Earth to reappear as chaotic disruptions. This is one reason that working with dark energies requires great care. The balance needs to be maintained, and when released, you should direct it into something that can make positive use of the energy, or ask the Lady and the Lord to guide you in this matter.

Psychology of Magic

In the first chapter I mentioned that all magic begins in the mind, and that all we know must first be defined by the mind in order for it to be known. This identification process is one of the ways the brain functions, sometimes with leaps of insight, at other times through synaptic connections deliberately created and practiced until the connection becomes a natural bridge. There is evidence that in some early civilizations, the color blue was not recognized except as a shade of green. Today we hear people state that black is the absence of color rather than a color, or that there is no such thing as black hair, only deep shades of brown. How we come to recognize colors is a matter of synaptic development. How we come to use magic is another such development.

From the psychological point of view, the subconscious mind is where all activities first take place. Because of the workings of neural transmitters and the distance run by nerve impulses, even when short-circuited at the spinal cord for immediate response, the reality is that the conscious mind is only *remembering* what has already taken place. This is due to the necessary time lag between an event and a person's cognitive awareness of that event. Indeed, a connection may eventually be made between this process and the déjà vu ("already seen") experience. Déjà vu—that perception of having already experienced something while it is happening—is a characteristic that I associate with a developing subconscious awareness. This would mean that people with the ability to process preconscious stimuli and hold onto it are able to then alter events before they register on the conscious mind of other people. I will give a case in point, and I am sure that there are many people who can offer numerous additional examples.

When I was in my first year of college, and my brother was in his third year of college, we all got together at home for dinner one weekend. This was quite an event since we both lived on campus, and there was a lot of conversation going on at the dinner table. During the dessert of homemade cherry pie, my brother bit painfully into a cherry pit. This was when this particular deja vu experience began for me. I knew what his comment would be, I knew what my father would say, and I knew what I would quip. And most of all, I knew that my harmless remark would trigger a terrible argument between my father and brother, resulting in my brother leaving the table and driving back to college in a fury.

The scene unfurled exactly as I knew it would, but when it came time for me to make my remark, and I really *wanted* to make it, I forced myself to remain quiet. At that point, the conversation abruptly stopped at the table, and everyone turned their heads and looked at me! I remained silent, and they all seemed puzzled, then resumed their conversations in other directions. The dangerous episode had passed unremarkably because I retained awareness of the *subconscious* events and changed them, thus they never manifested as *conscious* events, registering to everyone else only as a strange interlude. My mother later asked me about the pause and what I had done, because she was certain she could recall an argument that never took place, so of course I could let her in on it.

Because all that the conscious mind is aware of is really past tense, you can use your developing talents to literally change history and manipulate time. With a little practice, and that sensation of kenning, you can dip into time and stretch it out so that you are never late arriving at a destination. In the working of magic, you quiet the conscious mind and let the subconscious mind become the active principle. The drumming, breathing, chanting, and dancing during the raising of energy acts to move you into an altered state, sometimes called an alpha state. Drugs and alcohol are not acceptable for achieving an altered state simply because these act to inhibit your awareness. When working magic, you are actually allowing the subconscious mind to create the reality that will then be perceived by the conscious mind, and that is why planning may be valuable in spell work, but not imperative. You can make your decisions on the spur of the moment as events require.

Part of magic and Witchcraft is not only using the power of an altered state in which your subconscious mind manifests reality to your conscious mind, but also trusting and using your intuition. If you feel you are in a dangerous situation, you can project a subconscious "keep away" persona to avert the danger. Body language is one of the factors used by criminals to select their victims, looking for signals that may be interpreted as fearfulness, confusion, or timidity. If your intuition tells you to avoid a situation, heed it—there is no point in being connected as a Witch if you are going to ignore the communications. By anticipating events, you can prepare for them or avert them.

In looking at the function of the subconscious mind in creating magic, we see the active principle of *manifesting reality*. All that we know and can know must first be thought of to be known. This is also why visualization is important. You need to be able to clearly see the result you are trying to manifest, otherwise the result of your magic will be as hazy as your vision. Here is where many people run into unexpected difficulty from cultural training. If all of your life you have been told that only the meek inherit the earth, that a rich man does not deserve to go to Heaven, that to be a good woman you must be obedient and subservient, then unless you can let go of those inhibitions, you will block yourself on the subconscious level when working magic to get a promotion, get a pay raise, or run your own business.

One reason I emphasized the need to be aware of your surroundings is to open those synaptic connections and train them to function automatically. When you first start being deliberately and actively aware, you will find that over a short period of time, more and more details of your environs will leap out at you. You may wonder where your mind has been all these years! Suddenly you realize that there are birds you never saw before living near you, wildlife of all sorts may start appearing around your yard, and you will feel *witchy*, meaning that you are sensing your oneness with Nature. Why? Because your subconscious awareness is being manifested and this will touch the subconscious awareness of wildlife, registering as "safe" and inviting since you are actually *looking* for them in a peaceful state of mind. This is an amazing feeling.

One of my favorite photographs is of my daughter training her little brother on how to communicate with wildlife. She was ten and he was three at the time when they approached a group of rabbits in a wilderness park. My son rushed out at the rabbits and away they ran. Then my daughter explained to him that you have to get down on the ground, be silent, and see yourself as rabbit. Following her lead, he did as she did, and in a few moments all the rabbits returned, coming right up to them both nose to nose, and that is the scene in the photograph. They both focused on the subconscious image of being rabbit, while letting their conscious awareness of being human children fade into the background, then projected the subconscious image to the rabbits, who came to see who these new rabbits were.

Once you start utilizing your subconscious mind, programming it to spot the unexpected, you will also begin tapping into what is called the Universal Unconscious. This leads us to the concept that there is universal knowledge available in a timeless mental plane. In this plane, everything that can be known is already known, and you may access this information with your subconscious mind, usually through meditation. By bringing the subconscious to the front through an alpha or altered state of awareness, you enter the realm of ideas and open the floodgates to creativity, and this is one of the many uses for meditation.

Meditation in Magic

Meditation is one of the first aspects of the Craft to work on to learn about focusing energy. One of the primary functions of meditation is to calm your mind and open your reception to desired energies. This practice can ease you into an altered state of awareness so that you can seek the answers to questions, receive guidance, and bring creative energies into yourself (see Class 3 in *Green Witchcraft III*). Meditation also aids you to interconnect with the various aspects of the Earth, be these animal, plant, mineral, or atmospheric. Creative meditations open you to communication with the Divine, and may be utilized for the arts and sciences, or as an offering of song or poetry to the Goddess and the God. The practice of meditation helps in your magical work through training your mind to reach an alpha state and developing your envisioning skills. You should try to meditate at least three times a week, but for optimal growth every day is best.

Find a time when you will not be disturbed for at least half an hour (later you will be able to meditate for a mere ten to twenty minutes to receive answers, or an hour for journey or relaxation meditations), perhaps lighting a candle and incense, playing some soothing and unobtrusive music on a tape or CD, and even casting a circle around your meditation area for a peaceful and undisturbed setting. Sit comfortably in a chair with your feet flat on the floor, or sit on the floor on a cushion or rug, keeping your back straight, and your hands at rest either on your knees or in your lap. Close your eyes and relax, then gather the tensions, excess and static energies from around your body, and with a blessing let these drain away into the floor or ground through your feet.

Begin a meditation with a simple breathing exercise that will help you relax. By focusing on a candle or on the rise and fall of your abdomen as you breathe, it will be easier to let your extraneous thoughts filter away. Take a deep breath to the count of two, hold it for a count of two, release it to a count of two, hold for a count of two, then repeat. You only need to do this two or three times to clear your lungs and settle into the meditation. You may want to try inhaling through your nose and exhaling through your mouth to get out any stale air accumulated at the bottom of your lungs. Next, begin envisioning what you consider a secure, comfortable place, perhaps a small dry cave, a burrow, a temple, a forest clearing, a little fortress, a castle. Build this safe place up, layer by layer, seeing the area around it, the path you take to get to it, and adding clearer features to it every time you meditate, so that it becomes keenly defined and real for you and can act as the starting point for any travels. The more you use this place, the easier it will be to arrive there. While it is not necessary to have a question to ask, if you do have one, prepare yourself with a single word or very short phrase to release once you are fully relaxed. To end the meditation, take a deep breath and exhale. Do so again, letting the meditation depart. Take a third breath, inhaling the sense of all being right in the world. Exhale and you are back in normal consciousness. Ground yourself by touching the floor and letting any residual energy drain away, then have something to eat or drink, or move back into a daily routine. You may want to keep a journal of your meditations to keep track of your development.

Another meditation technique uses chanting or drumming, which continues until the alpha state is reached. At that time, the chanting or drumming may cease of its own accord. Prayer beads are often used in conjunction with chanting, usually beads with a single tassel at the start/finish point are fingered as the beads are passed along, each one cueing a chant. You can make your own, using forty beads for a bracelet-size circle or as many as 108 for a necklace size loop, or look for the sandalwood or seed prayer beads used in Hinduism and Buddhism. Chants and mantras may be anything you desire, or you may adopt a more familiar one, such as "Aum Namah Shivaye," "Hare Krishna," or simply "Om." But the chant may be related to what you seek, such as, "Love and Light," "Peaceful Bliss," or "I Am _____" and fill in the blank with the appropriate word (healthy, happy, joyful, worthy, etc.), or repeating the name of the deity image that has meaning for you, such as "Hecate, Hecate," or "Herne, Herne," or a repetition of the various deity names that you associate with such as, "Isis, Diana, Cerridwen, Hecate, Innana"; "Kali, Astarte, Hecate, Morrigan"; "Shiva, Hades, Herne, Cernunnos." Bring your chant from deep inside—from your diaphragm rather than from your throat—with a low rumbling tone, and this will keep your breathing right for meditation. The chanting or drumming draws the mind's focus to the restful, repetitive sounds, and moves you into the meditation and altered state. With a meditative mind, you can also discover a personal mantra or chant.

By steady, focused breathing, chanting, or drumming, you silence the conscious mind. Once you have achieved a restful state, you may address the purpose of the meditation if you have one. If you are working on problem-solving or creativity, now is the time to focus on a word or a question that needs an answer. You may want to use a guided meditation, which you can buy already recorded, or read and tape your own to play once you feel relaxed and receptive. A guided visualization helps you to enter an altered state and shows you that time, space, and what is considered reality exist only as you perceive them to be, so they are not limitations and boundaries, but are unlimited or even non-existent as you choose.

When you use tarot cards, a crystal ball, black mirror, runes, tea leaves, and other forms of divination, you are accessing other planes through a light meditative state. The process switches off the routine consciousness, freeing the subconscious or intuitive mind to view the stimuli of the card images, the depth of the crystal ball, the arrangement of tea leaves, and so on. Through this opening, you are able to draw in new information and new approaches to problems and life situations. Divination shows how things are currently lined up and that this can be changed, meaning that by tapping into this information, you now have the opportunity to direct the course of events as already discussed, through creative visualization and manifesting your subconscious.

7

Components of Spell Crafting

Bringing in the Elementals

Before you can cast a spell, you must first craft it, rather like a musician must first compose a symphony before it can be played at the public concert hall. Witchcraft is both religion and craft—a sacred art form in which you express yourself and interact with energies, spirits, and Divine Power on a personal level, thus making your spell work a very personal art form. The tables of correspondences in your BOS help you to keep a record of what works for you, and these tables are revised and altered according to results. Do not be surprised if a symbolic representation that another person finds useful fails to work for you. This happens because we are each unique and our perceptions of the Universe will vary according to how our minds and spirits function in relation to the stimuli of correspondences. There are people who cannot imagine why the color yellow is associated with Air, for example, and they see instead white, light blue, or red as more appropriate. The colors you use

depend upon your ability to make the association, so you will indeed make revisions as needed. Always trust your intuition in these matters as this is your connection to the Universe and is what makes your distinct signature art in the Craft. By keeping a journal, you can then track your success rate with various associations.

The active components of your spell crafting will center around some basic correlations, which will differ with Traditions and individual practitioners. With time and active practicing of your Craft, you will find it easier to relate your spell actions and procedures to the Elemental associations that will aid in your manifesting of changes. Earth may be seen as physicality, strength, stability, north, green, and black. You could relate Earth to magical procedures using stones, crystals, herbs, sachets, pillows, and poppets. Air may be seen as respiration, intellect, creativity, east, yellow, and red, with the related magics of chanting, breath work, meditations, channeling, rhyming, and anything that uses feathers, clouds, smoke, or incense work. Fire may be seen as life-energy, drive, passion, south, red and white, with related magics being such things as candle spells, energy raising, and the burning of spell materials such as herbs, woods, and inscribed papers. Water may be seen as vital fluids, blood, emotion, intuition, west, blue, and gray, with the related magics of cleansings, scrying, divination, teas, use of particular types of water such as spring, well, river, or storm water as washes and consecrated waters, and the emotion-driven spells of love and dreams.

The Elemental listings in Appendix A offer a starting point for further developing your own associations, but in any spell casting you will most likely be working with a combination of Elemental aspects. As an example, you could say that the spell using Air for cleansing smoke also has Fire, for this is what creates the smoke. However, the important factor in the smoke is that it is in motion, an attribute of Air, and thus, as with incense, the cleansing properties move through that Elemental.

The last of the colors listed above for each of the Elementals (black, red, white, and gray) are attributed to traditional Celtic culture, but these associations may not work for you under every circumstance, and so you may find your colors change according to the type of magic you are creating. Perhaps the Celtic ones will only appeal to you when you are working with Crone and Hunter aspects of the Divine, but any object used in spell crafting has at least one readily apparent Elemental association for you to draw upon for empowerment of the item. Most objects can be related to all the Elementals, with the emphasis being determined by the purpose and method of your spell work. Pottery, as an example, is made of clay material from Earth, that has been molded with Water, in a creative design of Air, and baked in a kiln of Fire, but you could focus on the Earth relationship in your spell crafting.

Throughout I have referred to the Four Elementals, but there are those who consider Spirit to be a fifth Elemental. I did not grow up with this concept, and so I do not use it in my own practice, primarily because my mother considered the Spirit to be our connection with the Divine, rather than an Elemental *aspect* of the Divine. We share Spirit with Divinity and with each other, hence the importance of not harming one another lest we will harm ourselves in Spirit. The alignment of the Elementals with the hands and feet of the human body places Spirit at the top with the head, where the crown chakra is located, and where it completes the pentagram symbol. The center space of the pentagram is the conduit, as it were, between the worlds as with the midhe of an ogham casting, through which the power is passed to us and released from us. This is one reason why the pentacle is an important tool in spell casting, for it is the representation on your altar in wood, tile, or metal of the pentagram with the central conduit. The spell materials are set in the center of the pentagram as you raise, focus, direct, and release energy so that the Power is passed into it and directed from it through the center for manifestation.

Constructing the Spell with Correspondences

In creating your spells, you incorporate a variety of the correlations listed in your BOS. Besides the Elemental associations, you have those of herbs, colors, Moon phases, days and hours, planetary arrangements, and astrological events. With herbs and plants, you again have subassociations relating to the part of the plant you are using—leaves, stems, flowers, or roots—and the type of plant being used—trees, shrubs, vines, fruits, or nuts. The plants themselves may be light or dark focused, and some of these plants may be used with either focus according to your need. Additionally with color, besides the primary colors you have the subassociations of shadings, blended colors, and combinations of colors, as with a variegated candle or a chakra candle with seven layers of color. Lunar associations are generally confined to new, waxing, full, waning, and dark phases, but may also include astrological events as a subassociation for eclipses and the passage of the same phase (full—Blue Moon, or dark—Sidhe Moon) twice in a solar month. Timing may be determined by the association of hour of the day according to sunrise and sunset, as well as by the meaning of the day of the week, by deity, or by any other symbolism that aids in your focus.

To put your spells together, you select the components from your menu of correspondences to create a magical working. The first step in the process is to determine your goal—bringing peace into the home, as an example. If the goal is not clear to you—perhaps being only a vague awareness that you feel something needs to be done—then meditate on the matter, seeking the source of the reason for your spell crafting. From this you can now extrapolate your purpose, which in our example would be the repelling of negative energies. Next you are ready to decide your method—directive, as an example, censing the house to gather negativity and send it out the back door, followed with a sprinkling of crumbled loosestrife leaves around the baseboards of the rooms. In this example, the energies of frankincense and the herbs affect the energies in the room.

Because there are a variety of approaches to any given situation, the magic created will vary with the practitioner. The lists of correspondences help you to bring together energies to achieve your goal, giving you a selection of ingredients as it were. You determine what approach you want to use, then you construct the ritual and/or spell. You create your incantations—the words you will speak as you conduct the magic—keeping your goal, purpose, and method in mind, and keeping all aspects of your magical event consistent with these. Wording may be very straightforward, or as poetic as you like. The main thing to consider is that you are clear on your intent, and that you are comfortable with these words. Too many *thee's, thou's,* and *ye's* may trip up your tongue, so I recommend sticking to the language you know and understand.

As you raise energy, keep your focus so that you are able to gather the energy, direct it, and send it to accomplish the task you have set for it. Once the energy is sent, you must see the task as accomplished, which is traditionally done with an emphatic statement of the words, "So Mote It Be!" (SMIB). This is not to say that every sentence you utter need be followed by SMIB, and it is distracting if you overuse the expression. When you write out your spell, read it over to see how it sounds to your inner ear. Always show respect for the Divine and the Elementals, and learn to discern the shadings of the SMIB phrase so that you never come across as commanding the Goddess and the God or the Elementals—you would not like it if your family ordered you around, so you must have a care in how you speak to your Divine Family.

The Power of Words

This "So Mote It Be!" expression, so often used in the Craft, has a specific meaning, with the first letter of each word written in spells and expressed verbally in capitalized letters to emphasize their importance. Together they mean that what you are creating must come into being—not *please*, not *maybe*, but **must**, because you are creating the change, you are manipulating (in the positive sense of *moving*) the energy. There is no room for doubt or pleading in the conducting of magic—if you are uncertain or hesitant, you diminish the energy and contradict yourself. When you state these words, you are making a declaration to the Universe, with the love of the Goddess and the God around you, and with the assistance of the Elementals in the passing of this magical event. To not affirm the magic is to not affirm them.

Many times you will want to preface your SMIB with, "As I Will," followed by, "So Mote It Be." The import here is that you are manifesting your personal will, through magic. There are many practitioners who preface the SMIB with a statement to the effect: "As I will and it brings harm to none," followed by the SMIB. To me, this diminishes your self-confidence in knowing what you are doing and "working in perfect love and perfect trust." Witchcraft is very empowering, and some people are not comfortable with this, perhaps retaining a cultural fear of being in control of their own destinies. For them, the Craft is fraught with imagined dangers, and perhaps the caveat of adding the "no harm" phrase helps them through a spell, but I feel it can also siphon off some of the raised energy, muting the power. You should be able to make the judgment as to whether or not you are doing something harmful.

Not everything you do in a ritual needs to be punctuated with a SMIB statement, but there are times when this phrase is used in the context of *affirmation* of unity, as when you might want to say that you are one with the Elementals for as they are part of you in body, breath, energy, and blood, so are you part of them, SMIB—with the meaning that this is how it is, that there is connection and there must be balance. This is also expressed with, "As above, so below" and in the medieval Christian philosophical admonition that God and the Devil are the inverse of the same being (the polar opposites of one Divinity as it were). Do not be hesitant nor bland in your speaking voice, but expressive as you would be in ordinary conversation with people whose company you enjoy and around whom you are comfortable. It is okay to laugh, and there is no need to speak everything in a monotone.

The words you speak during the ritual ought to flow for you— thus the long version of the Rede included the recommendation that spells be spoken in rhyme. The rhythm of sounds impresses the mind with a sense of the spell words being out of the ordinary, and while some of it may be pure doggerel and sing-song, the point is not to produce award-winning poetry. The rhyming of your spell words also acts as a memory aid, so that if you are repeating a particular spell periodically, you will come to remember the words. This is a technique with an ancient history and forms the basis of oral mythic and religious traditions in many cultures.

The wording of spells should encompass the different acts you are performing and name the ingredients while citing their function in the spell. This narrows the focus of the energies you are working with, keeping everything flowing in the same direction. Be careful not to let your words wander so that instead of being focused, you are rambling, and thus scattering the energy you have been gathering. All the materials used in spell work are blessed by you as you go through the magic process, so that if using mugwort, as an example, to brew a wash for your crystal ball you will first say something along the lines of, "I bless thee mugwort that thy energies work well for me." Then as you add the hot water to the herbs in a bowl resting on the pentacle, you will make a statement of the particular function of the herb such as, "I call upon you mugwort to aid in my divinations." Here you would be holding your palms over the brew to transmit that energy, and when the wash had cooled enough for use, you proceed to gently wash the crystal ball or black mirror. At this point you are moving into another phase of the ritual, and you would address the energies to the object, such as by saying, "May this wash of blessed mugwort cleanse and awaken the energies for divination in this_____."

Outlining your spell, gathering the ingredients together, constructing your words, be they sentences, a chant, or a set of rhymes, and planning each step of the way will ensure a smooth spell casting. There are people who warn that it is imperative to verbally nail down every corner of a spell, defining it with exact precision lest the spell go awry, and even ending it with words that it not turn on you, but my feeling on this is that such worries only lessen your power. You know that you are working with the Divine and the Elementals, and you should maintain that "Perfect Love and Perfect Trust" that they will watch over you and aid you in your casting. The idea of the need for a precision of words, accompanied by a fear of an unexpected backlash, is something that has seeped into Witchcraft from ceremonial magic associations. This fearfulness can in turn be traced to the Vedic Aryan practices of India where if one word is misspoken in a ritual, the whole ritual must be started over from the beginning (which could bankrupt a person), lest the purpose of the ritual fail. The whole point of this concept was to institutionalize a caste of people in a position of superiority, because only the priestly order of Brahmans know the "right" words to speak. This tradition of exactitude has passed into the Judaic tradition with the Levites being the priestly caste of the Hebrews who know the right words for rituals, and into Christian formulae more readily apparent in Catholic practices. Part of "Perfect Love and Perfect Trust" is knowing that your Divine Mother and Father, and your sibling Elementals are not going to maliciously harm you—they understand your intent. And conversely, the Divine and the Elementals will work very hard to keep you from harming yourself, unless it is a lesson you insist on learning.

The intuitive connection works both ways, so that not only are you receiving information, but you are transmitting information, and the Universe will hear you. The spell materials are tools that aid in your focus, but these are not the end all of magic. If you fear the process of magic, if you believe that one misstated word will throw everything into disarray, if you fear that your own magic will turn on you like some grade-B horror movie, then you are not operating with "Perfect Trust," and you need to address this issue before attempting magic. What do you fear? Why do you fear? These are questions you should ask in a meditation when you are in a secure meditative place (an example of this type of meditation is on page 16 of *Green Witchcraft II*). You must trust the Divine and the Elementals to understand.

There are people who speak their words in their minds rather than by voice, and while this will work, my personal feeling is that the power of the spoken word is traditional to the magic of manifestation. Uma Parvati, the Mother Goddess of India, whose consort is Shiva, is also known literally as the power of the spoken word, and in Judeo-Christian tradition, God speaks the creation, while in the New Testament, the lineage of Jesus is described as evolving from the *Word* (Gospel of John) that was *with* God and that *was* God. Throughout magical traditions in all cultures, the power of the spoken word is acknowledged, so I do recommend that if you are shy about speaking out loud, even when spell casting as a Solitary Witch, you should address this issue as well. Find out what it is that makes you afraid to speak up, then face the problem and defeat it. You could be quite surprised at the source of the matter. Were you told that good children are quiet children? Were you criticized or ridiculed as you grew up whenever you offered an opinion? Meditation will help you find the source of your fear so you can conquer it.

Vital to the crafting of any spell is a clear understanding of just what it is that you want to accomplish, and your words should be consistent with that goal and purpose. Do not just rush into spell casting unless you have a clear idea as to what you want, remembering that spells take ideas and turn them into physical manifestations. As discussed earlier, the Rules of Conduct and/or the Witches' Rede are ethical standards available to you as an ethical and moral base for your practice. If you find that you are having difficulty coming up with the words to use for your spell, you may need to revise your focus. Walk through the spell, changing things as necessary so that the ritual event flows smoothly and feels natural to you.

The Craft Name

Another component of your practice is your Craft Name. This is the magical name you chose for yourself and wear when conducting magic. Such a name is primarily drawn from what is of interest to you or what attracts you. If, as an example, the cry of the redwing blackbird thrills you, you might want your magical name to be Redwing. If your focus is on herbs, you could choose your name from among your favorites, such as Anise, Damiana, Elderflower, Thyme, or Rosemary. You could select a name for the correlation you draw from it, so that if you seek more courage, you could call yourself Valkyrie, Dragonfire, or other such name that implies this attribute to you. If you want to emphasize your desire to learn, you could call yourself by a name that conveys this meaning to you, such as a variation on Searcher, Seeker, or Huntress, or an animal that relates to learning, such as Owl or Bear.

The selection of your magical name may be derived from historic or mythic names, or variations of these names—which makes it more your name rather than simply borrowing someone else's. While borrowing a name may be seen as a compliment or a demonstration of attunement to an individual or a characteristic of that person you seek to emulate, you need to ensure that the name relates to you in some special way—otherwise you may end up being one of five Rhiannons at a Pagan Gathering. Hence, many people will add something to the borrowed Goddess name, so that Rhiannon becomes Rhiannon Ravenwing or Rhiannon Silverwheel. The important thing about having a magical name is that when you assume it for spell crafting, it sets you apart from the mundane routine, triggering the message to your subconscious that magic is about to begin, and so you identify yourself to the Divine, the Elementals, and the Universe when you state your Craft name just prior to casting the circle:

I draw this circle in the presence of the Goddess and the God where they may come and bless their child, _____.

A magical name may be used around other like-minded persons, and is frequently the name given in introduction at Pagan gatherings and festivals. The more you use this name in conjunction with your magical practice and associates, the more it will become infused with the magical persona you wish to project. It is a name that can be used to provide you with anonymity in any setting, and yet will become a familiar name for those you commune with in the Craft, so that these people will see you as that name. There are many people who have become so closely connected with their Craft name that they have brought this name into their mundane world so that they might more fully live their Craft. That being said, choose your name with care so that you may wear it comfortably.

You may fine-tune the energy rhythms of your Craft name by using numerology to match the number of your name with your birth date, called your path number. In Appendix A, there is a numerology chart listing the number association for each letter of the alphabet. Write out your birthday in numbers by month (1 through 12), day, and year, then add the numbers and reduce to the most basic digit. Next, create your Craft name, adding or subtracting letters so that the numerological value of your name matches your path number. This will help the energy to flow easiest for you.

Craft names may change over time, but if you find you are going through one name after another, you probably need to be more focused when choosing a name. New names may be selected upon entering a coven, being then a Coven name, and then there is also what is called a Working name. This latter name is a secret name the Witch creates for magical workings, and may indeed be the same as the Craft name if no one else knows it. But if the Craft name is known throughout a Pagan community, as an example, then the Witch will use the Craft name in public rituals, but the Working name in private spell work. The old Working name may be released from use upon a dedication ritual, since one of the things that happens during this ritual is that the Goddess and the God tell you what your secret name is—usually a word that "defines" you. This now becomes the Working name, and is revealed to no one, for it is your link with the Divine.

Tools for the Spell

With the Green Craft, the tools of the practice most often come directly from Nature, so that a wand may be simply a sturdy twig, a cauldron might be a shell or the husk of a coconut, and so forth. I have seen the long trencher-like pods of date palms used as libation bowls, and seed pods used to hold the blessed water and salt. I have picked up from fallen wood a bushy twig, leafy or with evergreen needles on it, to sweep the circle, and then returned the tool to Nature with my blessing when finished. A long stick lying on the ground is sanctified by blessing it as you hold it and present it to the Elementals and the Divine, invoking their blessings to empower the tool for use as a wand or a stang with which the circle might be delineated. The gifts of Nature are always acceptable tools, and so you need not expend a lot of money for Craft accouterments.

Anything that you gather in the open from Nature is blessed by its immediate contact with its natural surroundings. Thus if you are doing an outside ritual and pick up a stick to use as your wand, merely presenting it to the Quarters and the Divine, stating what it is, will make it ready for your work. The important part of magical tools is the energy that you channel into them. If using stones at the Quarters or as part of your spell work, you may want to wash them or sprinkle them with spring water or running water, such as from a creek, river, or the sea. Being inventive and creative with the tools collected on site is part of the art of the Craft.

The most commonly used tools in spell crafting are the ritual broom (besom) for clearing the circle space (never used for house-work), the wand for invocations and directing energy, and the caul-dron for holding the spell ingredients as they are used. These are the most basic Witchcraft tools, and these can be found in Nature, made, or purchased. When working in Nature, drawing the penta-gram on the ground will take care of the pentacle tool, or if indoors, you can even simply draw it on a piece of paper and set your caul-dron on top of it. Other tools used in the crafting of spells are the ritual knife, or athame (a-tham´me, a-thaw´me, ath´a-may, and a-thawm´ being among the many variations of pronunciations) used in consecration and directing energy, and the working (or cutting) knife, called the bolline (bo-leen´) used to carve, cut, and inscribe. The athame is often a black-handled, double-edged knife, much like a dagger, while the bolline is white- or brown-handled with a single cutting edge, rather like a pocket knife. The bolline may also have a crescent blade and be dedicated to cutting herbs. I have two bollines, using the white-handled one in spell work and the brown-handled crescent one for gathering herbs. While you might also like to utilize the different styles of bolline, it is merely a matter of pref-erence and certainly not a requirement.

Some people are uncomfortable with using a tool that has been pre-owned, but many others enjoy browsing rummage sales, thrift shops, and antique stores for their tools. Getting a second-hand item is perfectly fine, so long as you cleanse the item of prior energy influences and consecrate it to work for you. Keep newly cleansed

121

and consecrated tools with your other tools in an area that affords them protection from negative energies, while allowing them to become imbued with your own energies. Some people like to keep their tools around their living spaces or in a magic room or area, and this helps to infuse the tools with their energies. I have done this myself with some items, such as the chalice and pentacle, and find that it adds to the comfort of working with them. If for any reason it is not suitable for you to have tools where someone else might see them, then by all means, keep them tucked away, usually cloaked in black cloth.

The one important rule about tools is that you do not handle those belonging to other people unless they invite you to. I consider it rude to even ask for permission, as this puts the person in the embarrassing position of having to say no and worrying about hurting your feelings, or to say yes possibly under duress and discomfort. Always cleanse tools that have been handled by other people. Remember, too, that in touching someone's magical equipment, you may be drawing into yourself some of their energy, and that may not always be to your advantage.

Ritual Jewelry

Jewelry is another type of tool. We often have very personal energies wrapped around our ritual jewelry, and so again, never reach out for someone's pendant, bracelet, or ring without permission. A ring is often a symbol of initiation, dedication, or elevation in a degree system, and as such is to be as respected as a wedding ring. My feeling about rings is that if you have a dedication (et al) ring, it should remain on your finger rather than being set aside for whatever reason—but that is just my personal approach to rings that I picked up from my mother. Like her, my rings have over the years become unremovable unless they are cut off. Pendants, however, are the usual victim of the unthinking grab by others, and if this happens to you, at the first opportunity, cleanse and reconsecrate the piece.

The purpose of jewelry may vary from adornment, artistic energy, and expression, to the magical properties of crystals and stones, personal attunement with the Lady and the Lord of the Craft, and identification among others of like mind. Symbology is associated with different types of jewelry, and what may be appropriate for one Tradition may not be for another, but no one has the corner on what you as an individual and practitioner of the Craft may or may not wear unless you accept this through a coven connection. The independent spirit of the Witch does not evaporate because someone makes a declaration about a piece of jewelry, be it an amber and jet necklace or a garter.

The idea of reserving the use of a garter with buckles to show how many covens have formed (hived) from yours is a questionable one, since garters are decorative adornments used by anyone—for centuries everyone wore garters to hold up their hose. It has become popular in some Traditions to suggest that in England, the Order of the Garter was formed to prevent a Lady from being dishonored when her blue (or some say red) garter slipped off during a royal ball, thus identifying her as a practitioner of the Old Religion. I have a hard time accepting that tale, first because green would have been more likely a Craft color, since it was associated in that time with Fairie and Witchcraft, and second because the founding of the Order is documented in the Chronicles of Froissart. Indeed, garters of all colors were the fashion rage at the time of the incident and decorated everything from legs to jackets to bedposts. The Order of the Garter, which consists of twenty-four appointed companion knights to the king (or queen) was founded in 1348 by Edward III and is based out of the Windsor chapel of Saint George. This order of chivalry was founded when a garter was dropped by a virtuous lady during a dance. The king picked up the garter, and said "evil to him who sees evil in this" or "there is no evil in this," because, according to the medieval source, while the king was known to be enamored of the married lady, he had never touched her, hence, she had not deliberately dropped the garter to attract his attention.

The use of the amber and jet necklace may be designated as only High Priestess attire by some Traditions, but anyone—including non-Wiccans—can purchase such a necklace in a store or from a catalog. To the coven members of a particular Tradition this might be a matter of official designation, but to anyone else it is not. Amber and jet are nonmineral, the first being plant resin that is millions of years old, and the second being carbon-based and also ancient. Therefore, anyone who works with Nature and who feels the connection of energy through time would be in tune with the energies of amber and jet, and can use these energies to enhance the power of their magical workings (amber) and to bind the raised energies to the work until the goal is achieved (jet). Wearing amber and jet is indicative of working with and being connected with Nature through the practice of Witchcraft, but again, it could just be decorative jewelry.

Crystals are often chosen for wearing according to desired characteristics they represent. Enhancing your own energies with those of selected crystals may be done with bracelets, rings, pendants, earrings, or simply placing the crystals on the altar or including them in the spell material. I have seen people who are simply draped in crystals, and it sounds like a cacophony of energies to me with a multitude of conflicting and overlapping vibrations. Not all of your ritual jewelry needs to be worn at the same time—some items are more attuned to special events (Full Moon, Sabbats, divination, spell casting, etc.) than others, and you should try to learn which ones these are.

Working the Energy

It is not enough to have all the ingredients to your spell ready and to know what you are going to say if you are unable to work with energies. There are the subtle energies of devas found in herbs and plants, and there are the Elemental energies invoked for the aspects of the essences of life. Spirit energies may also be called upon to aid in work, and these act as guides and helpers. Your own spirit is part of the magical process since, in the Green practice, you are drawing the Earth energy into yourself when you ground and center, and you are also raising energy from a variety of sources, all of which are focused through you to be released to accomplish a goal—energies you generate outwardly. This latter event is typical in healings, particularly when using the palms of your hands. Personal energy radiates from you, and can be seen in your aura. This may be enhanced or augmented by indrawn energies for working magic.

Your use of psychic energies occurs in your relationship with your surroundings. It is through your psychic energy that your intuition functions, bringing input to your subconscious mind about the energy fields and auras located around you or around an area. This sensitivity may not necessarily be sought out, and this is why some psychic people see visions of events happening elsewhere to total strangers. The psychic energy is like your personal radar. The unconscious transmitting of that energy is an uncontrolled response to psychic stimuli or internal disorganization, usually caused by chemical and hormonal imbalance as is experienced in puberty, pregnancy, and menopause. This is static energy, being broadcast randomly and with neither intent nor goal. People have a difficult time with this type of energy surge, and counteracting it is very trying, but awareness of the situation is a healthy step in the right direction. Meditation on what triggers the psychic bursts may lead to methods of self-control or redirection of the energy into productive goals.

I tend to categorize psychic energy as *generally* receptive in nature, with input from energy sources around you being recognized and processed on the subconscious level. You utilize this energy when you address the herbs you need for spell work, when you look at a person's aura, and when you gather information about crystals and other objects. Unless uncontrolled bursts are being generated in response to stimuli, the energies you send outward are mingled with other energies. If you only send your personal energy out to accomplish goals, you will become drained and possibly very depressed. You need to deliberately bring outside energy inward to manipulate it, direct, and send it back out to do the task assigned.

On the subject of energy, some people confuse Fairies or Elementals with Thoughtforms, but this latter being is a type of energy that you create, shape and send out on a mission to fulfill one particular goal. Once the task is performed, the Thoughtform is released or allowed to dissipate. More than any other type of magic, this is filled with your own energy. If you create a Thoughtform for a task and want to keep it around to continue performing that task, you will need to "nourish" it with more energy, which comes from yourself through focusing your thoughts on it, visualizing the form and seeing it healthy and vital. With this energizing intent, you need to retain your health with proper eating habits and exercise, supplementing your own energy through grounding and centering, and bringing in Earth energy to assist you whenever you "feed" your Thoughtform, then releasing the excess energy. By bringing the Earth energy within, you are uniting with it, blending it into your own energies, and when finished, you are unblending the energies so the remaining Earth energy returns. All energy moves in cycles, and once the Thoughtform has completed the task, it too will be released into the Earth.

The most common use of a Thoughtform is for protection—alerting you to dangers, thus supplementing your intuition, but this form may also be very effective in finding things for you. If you work well with the Elementals, you might be less inclined to create a Thoughtform, putting your needs in the hands of your Elemental kith and kin instead—it all depends on your comfort level.

Spirit energies come to you in many forms. A familiar is a spirit energy in the form (usually) of an animal pet. Totem animals may appear to you in visions during times of need, and these are also spirit energies. When you channel with those who have passed on, you are contacting spirit energies, and these are often helpful as guides. With channeling, you will likely attract many spirits who are simply curious or chatty, while there may be others who have a message they want to convey to someone. By working through a spirit guide, you are shielding yourself from an overdose of energy stimuli that could leave you drained and depressed. My mother always said, "The spirits are good." But sometimes they take for granted your limitations unless a guide reminds them that you are tired and the session is over. A strong guide is one whose light is like the sun at noon, and this guide can effectively close a session if you are either unaware of your own limitations or fail to recognize your fatigue. Begin any channeling session by grounding and centering, end with grounding of residual energy, and having something to eat and drink that will put some carbohydrates back into your system.

Because we are all interrelated through energy, with the purity of energy defined in relation to the Divine, we are able to connect with and work with any energy. The focus of the energy as light or dark refers not to good or evil but to balance, as with the aspects of Divine, in which energy travels full circle or in a circuit. Good and evil are matters of personal intent; qualifiers of our own spiritual growth and evolution. We are not judged by any divine tribunal, where a book of misdeeds is read to you—we are judged by our inner selves, and some people impose a self-punishment on their spirit because they feel this will expiate their spirits for previous inadequacies.

You see people in life who are their own worst enemy, undercutting themselves every time they begin to succeed, and the underlying word to their behavior is "unworthy." One of the most difficult aspects of spiritual evolution is coming to the realization that you are indeed worthy, that you are indeed loved by the Divine, and that you can accept forgiveness for those actions you regret. The energy flow is the same either in Light or in Dark—and through the Dark you find healing and move into the Light. That is why the Underworld, Shadowland, or Summerland are places of spiritual repose, where the energies that have been misdirected may be renewed so that the spirit grows in strength and light. Passage then through the cauldron of rebirth provides an opportunity to take that light back into the physical realm to continue to grow or to help others in their life path.

Outlining Your Magical Work

No matter how many spells you collect, each time you perform a magical function it is a new event. You need to review the spell, outlining the components so that you do not leave things out or lose your focus. It is fine to have an outline on your altar as you work, and many diagrams of how to set up an altar leave a space at the center closest to the practitioner for the Book of Shadows or Spellbook. The propriety of this custom is even echoed in the placing of the book of the Mass for a Roman Catholic priest to read from while performing the Eucharist rituals at the altar. There are any number of formats you can follow for the event, but here is a listing that may help you prepare for your magical experience. This simple format may be adjusted as needed.

1. What is the purpose?

    a. Drawing

    b. Repelling (banishing/exorcising)

    c. Containing (deflecting/reflecting/returning to sender)

2. What is the goal?

    a. Bring _____ to me

    b. Cast _____ away from me

    c. Shield _____ by doing _____

3. What is the method?

    a. Sympathetic (this IS that)

    b. Comparative (this REPRESENTS that)

    c. Directive (this AFFECTS that)

    d. Transference (this ENTERS that)

4. What tools will be needed for the work?

    a. Wand

    b. Athame

    c. Cauldron

    d. Pentacle

    e. Salt

    f. Water

    g. Incense

    h. Matches

    i. Deity images/representations (candles, stones, etc.)

5. What materials will be used in the magic?

    a. Candles

    b. Herbs

    c. Material for making a poppet

    d. Stones/crystals/gems

    e. Natural materials (feathers, leaves, twigs, shells, etc.)

    f. Oils

    g. Paper and ink

    h. Sigils or symbols

    i. Cloth for sachets/pillows/poppets

    j. Container of water for potpourri

6. When will the event take place?

    a. Appropriate lunar phase

    b. Day of the week

    c. Hour of the day

7. What words will be used in the ritual?

    a. Statement of purpose_____

    b. Statement of goal_____

    c. Deities invoked_____

    d. Energies invoked_____

    e. Energy releasing word(s)_____

    f. Closing words_____

8. How will the energy be raised and moved?

    a. Chanting

    b. Dancing

    c. Breathing

    d. Gestures

9. What type of working will aid in the manifesting of the goal?

   a. Making a poppet or other image

   b. Making an herbal potpourri

   c. Knotting silk cords or yarn

   d. Inscribing a candle

   e. Burning herbs in a candle

   f. Making a talisman

   g. Consecrating an amulet

   h. Creating a charm

   i. Working with herbs as wreaths, swaths, strewn, etc.

This, then is the overview of the entire magical working with the above elements incorporated:

1. Choose the timing of the spell

2. Outline the ritual

3. Prepare the sacred space and have all equipment ready

4. Cleanse and purify self; ground and center

5. Purify the ritual area

6. Create the sacred space/cast the circle

7. Invoke the Elementals at the Quarters

8. Invoke the Goddess and the God

9. State the purpose for the ritual

10. Conduct the spell:

   a. Create the magical object/bring together the magical ingredients

   b. Raise energy

    c. Focus energy

    d. Direct the energy into the spell material

    e. Release the energy to manifest the goal

11. Ground residual energy

12. Celebrate Cakes and Wine

13. Bless and farewell the Powers

14. Open the circle

15. Clean up/put away tools/dispose of spell materials as needed

Casting the Spell

Once you have determined your purpose and goal, formulated the method and type of magic you want to conduct, put together your ingredients, constructed the procedure, decided on your wording, and fixed upon the timing, you then go through the actual casting of the spell. All that precedes the magical event is the crafting of the spell, but the event itself is when that spell is cast, or *performed*. This is when the energy is manipulated, when the directing takes place. It is also when you make the Divine connection for the purpose of achieving a goal.

    I consider it inappropriate to place Elemental candles on the altar simply because this focuses their energies on the altar space rather than in the circle where you are raising energy. This arrangement in a limited space is also very inconvenient as you have to reach over an Elemental candle to reach the material on the altar. The use of Elemental candles at the Quarters of the Circle is preferred, but not necessary. You could place at the Quarters something that symbolizes each of the Elementals, or you may invoke them with neither candles nor symbols used. You are inviting these energies to hold your circle, to lend their aid in your work, but they are already represented on the altar with salt or the pentacle, incense, candle, and water. When constructing your spell, you should have at least one candle that is designated for your magical or ritual working. The *working candle* is not the same as the Goddess and the God candles, and it is the one that is in the color related to the spell work—green for money, pink for love, and so forth, while the Deity candles may be white or colored according to the Deity image. The Goddess candle may be blue or green and the God candle may be orange or red for typical spell work, or candles may be used that are in alignment with the season (see ritual outlines in *Green Witchcraft*). At minimum, with a Wiccan altar you could have three candles, four if you include a candle to represent the Divine as One (which is usually white and is placed between the Goddess candle and the God candle).

There are a lot of spell books available today, and while it is likely that you can glean some ideas from them, the spells do not need to be copied exactly to be effective—in fact, I recommend changing at least one facet to make the spell your own. If you follow the wording and procedure exactly, you are essentially doing someone else's spell, and simply through that awareness you will probably send some of the raised energy to augment the energy of that person. Words are important, but they are not the end-all of a spell—*your* words are vastly more important than someone else's words.

Once the spell is cast, you must see it as accomplished. You no longer think about the need for the spell, the process of the spell, the crafting of the spell, but only see the outcome as a done deal. In this way, you are paving the road to manifestation, because before something can be known, it must first be thought of—and you are providing the thought impetus. There may be times when the result of the spell is not immediately manifested, in which case you may want to boost the spell with a shortened version of the original. If you are seeking a major change, you may need to send energy bursts periodically, such as by lighting a candle used in the spell for an hour every day for seven days, which is typical when using seven-day candles in a jar. If you feel that the spell did not work, you may need to reexamine the goal. Were you acting within the ethical guidelines of the Rules or the Rede? Were you attempting to evade a life-lesson you need to learn? Try meditating on where the spell was inadequate, and listen to what comes to you. Sometimes people subvert their own workings, either because they really do not believe they can make a change, or because they haphazardly threw together ingredients without a clear understanding of what energies they wanted to work with. When a spell does not work, it is usually because of one of these reasons, and refocusing may help you over-come the obstacles to cast a more appropriate spell.

Magical Practice

Candle Spells

Working spells with candles is one of the most common and effective magical practices, but there are some simple precautions that still need to be addressed. The first thing you will want to do is check the bottom of the candle. If you are using a votive-type candle (these are generally round, come in a variety of colors and scents, and range between 1 and 1½ inches tall), there is usually a paper sticker on the bottom of the candle. This needs to be peeled off so it won't catch fire later on. The votive style of candle is the easiest to find in any supermarket, gift shop, and card store, so it is the sort most often used in spell work, especially since you can coordinate the fragrance as well as the color into your energy raising. For spells that include the dropping of herbs into the candle flame, you need a suitable container—one that will not split or break from the additional heat. The container that works best is that typical tool of Witchcraft—a medium-size, footed metal cauldron (usually three feet). You will also need a heat-proof pad to set the cauldron on, which is why the use of a tile or wooden

135

pentacle is, in my opinion, better than a metal one. Metal will conduct the heat to the surface of your altar or working area rather quickly and could scorch the area.

If using a votive glass container, *never* hold the glass once the candle is melted, because it is extremely hot. Besides burning your fingers, you could drop the glass and spread burning hot wax, creating a fire hazard.

The cauldron you select for spell work might be made of metal alloys or of iron, and the larger the size of the container, the heftier it is to carry. For typical candle spells using herbs, a cauldron that sets on your altar may be between 5 and 6½ inches across the top and 3½ to 6½ inches deep. Anything smaller may not contain the melted wax of just an ordinary votive, while adding herbs would be a genuine fire hazard. The practice of the Craft is not about burning your house down. The main problem with a pottery cauldron, besides that of potential heat breakage, is that hot wax will seep through it and could stain the object it is sitting on. My favorite pottery one was made in Taos, New Mexico; it has Elemental designs impressed on the interior. It originally was a poured resin candle, which lent itself very nicely to a purification ritual for the later use of the cauldron as a Craft tool. While I do continue to use this, I am extra careful because I know what the associated problems are.

Not all candle spells require the addition of herbs, but I rarely work without them. After checking through your lists of correspondences in your BOS, your candle may be selected for the color, anointed with a suitable oil, inscribed with runic symbols, and simply lit during your spell ritual at the appropriate hour, day, and Moon phase. Do be careful when working with oils as they are also flammable.

Outline for yourself just what it is you want to do. You need to determine the focus of the spell for which the candle will be used, then looking over the list of correspondences, choose the candle color (and even its scent, since there are a lot of deliciously scented candles available) to match the focus. Decide what time of day and moon phase you want to use.

Select from your BOS lists an appropriate oil with which to dress the candle, then pick at the appropriate time the herbs you will use to enhance the power of the candle. Look over your list of runic symbols if you want to include these, and find which ones you want to inscribe on the candle. All this activity takes place as part of your outlining of your spell. You will want to have all the necessary ingredients together before you start the spell, and you may want to write out on a notecard or in your Spellbook what you are going to be doing, step by step. Here, too, you would include any timing considerations for the casting.

The list of correspondences for symbols will be used once your spell is completed to determine the likely outcome and time frame for this, based on any forms left in the spell materials and their placement in the cauldron or other container. With melted candle wax, there may be images present that can offer an interpretation. Use the edge of the container farthest from you on the altar as North, the closest as South; think of these regions as 12:00 and 6:00, for where the image lies may tell you when to expect the results to appear or how the spell will manifest. The East of the container is 3:00 and the West is 9:00, but these can be interpreted as days of the week, or weeks of the month as well. Often the symbols will simply verify to you that the spell has been effective, and not all of the symbols you see will be interpreted according to the listing. You have to use your intuitive powers to interpret the images in the wax, and that is part of what makes Witchcraft an art. Do not feel restricted to the meanings in any list of symbols if your instinct is telling you something else.

Once you have drawn your circle, made your invocations, and are ready to begin your spell, rub the candle with the oil(s) you have chosen to "dress" the candle. Some people feel that only the utility knife—the bolline—should be used for inscribing a candle, others like to use the athame, or ritual knife. I feel that the energy of the charged athame is more enhancing to spellwork than the bolline I use to cut herbs, willow branches, and so forth, and for me the athame is a magical tool that may be used in nonindustrial magical work. Inscribing a candle for magical use is not the same to me as etching symbols onto another tool such as the wand, so I use the athame for candle markings.

The symbols you draw into the candle can be placed around the candle side and if the candle is wide enough, on the top around the wick. You can use your own designs, runes, ogham markings, or any of the many "Witch alphabets" such as shown in *Buckland's Complete Book of Witchcraft*, by Raymond Buckland (Llewellyn Publications, 1993). The symbols used can be relevant to a magical focus (feoh— Ⱶ for wealth; sigel—Ⴉ for achievement; and wynn—Ᏼ for joy), or you can actually spell out the purpose of the candle spell (Bring Me Money). Some people like to insert a pin a little way down the candle with the intonation that when the candle burns to this level the spell is released. Another way to do this is to draw a line there. It is a matter of your own preference whether any of that is done—just having the symbols melt in the wax is sufficient to release the spell, and the markings may seem superfluous. I do not use pins in candles, simply because pins are so often used to contradict magic, as with a Witch's Bottle of sharp objects intended to deflect negative energy. Because I make this association, I feel they would be detrimental to a candle spell of my own making. Other people may not feel this connection as I do, and so for them, the use of pins in a candle works fine—this is why I remind you to follow *your* intuition; to do what feels right for you.

While you are working the candle, putting on the oils and symbols, you state what you are doing and why, maintaining your focus on the desired effect and visualizing it. See the power going into the candle as you put on the oil, see the effect occurring as you inscribe the candle, and by the end of the spell, you will envision the effect as done.

Spell work with candles is greatly enhanced with herbs chosen from your BOS list to fit the purpose. Always ask before gathering an herb, then bless the energies of the materials you have gathered and set on the altar for use before you start applying them to the spell work. Drop the selected herbs into the lighted candle one at a time, stating the name of the herb and the power you are drawing from it to work in the candle spell. You may have written a chant or a rhyme to speak as each item is added, or you may simply state something like, "basil for wealth, mint for money and blessing. . . ."

As you add herbs to the flame, feel the herbal energies moving into the spell. See the energies build in power, which you can aid at this point with dance, chant, and gesture, and when you feel the energy level is at the highest you can tolerate, release the energies by directing them to their purpose. Remember to use a short phrase or key word to send the power out to complete the spell. As soon as you send that energy to complete the task, see the spell as completed with the desired effect as attained.

Let the candle burn for an hour on the altar. That is all that is needed, but if you are feeling a sense of completion energy, you may want to let it burn longer. If you are doing spell work in conjunction with an Esbat, you could let the candle continue to burn as you complete that ritual, take some refreshment, ground (earth) the excess energy, open your circle, and put away your tools, except for the candle on the altar. Once the hour of candle burning ends, or longer if you feel the need, you may snuff out the candle, looking at any floating debris or images forming in the cooling wax for interpretation. Record what you see, perhaps drawing a little sketch for later reference, then dispose of the remaining used candle by burying it in earth or tossing it into moving water. When doing these spells with votive candles, there usually is not very much material left, which makes it easier to dispose of the remains. When you bury the remains in soil, you can repeat a little chant such as:

Here goes the seed into the fertile soil,
Let the spell grow with naught to foil.
That as I will, So Mote It Be!

Although most candle spells conclude with the proper discarding of the used candle remnants, some candles, especially those larger than votives, may be kept and relighted if dedicated to a purpose that can be renewed from time to time. A "money as I need it" focused spell or a running spell for good health are examples of renewable candle spells. For these, you would want to keep the candle wrapped in a cloth of the appropriate color and place it in a cupboard or drawer with your magic things so that you can retrieve it from time to time to set on the altar pentacle and relight on an appropriate day and hour—all of which comes from your BOS lists of correspondences. Another type of reuse happens when you burn a spell candle for a determined period of time to create the manifestation, perhaps moving the candle from one area to another as a demonstrative part of the ritual.

If no herbs were used in the candle, and only the top was inscribed, and then melted away, you may use the candle later on in a different spell. First you will need to terminate the original purpose from the candle itself through cleansing before you can use a candle again for a different spell. I only mention this practice as something that is possible, in an emergency perhaps, but I don't consider it a good idea to regularly reissue the same candle to different spells. I prefer to use the small votive candles for spells because they work well, they are not a big investment, and one candle suffices for one spell.

There are a number of different approaches to candle magics, and that is why they are so popular. While the versatility of candles is limited only by your imagination, a number of charming books on candle spells will prompt you with new ideas. Candles can be used in conjunction with other tools, such as being placed on either side of a black mirror, which may be propped up or lain flat on the altar during spell work. You can use different colors of candles and move them with symbolic meanings that you have ascribed to them and state as you proceed through the spell, such as indicating distance or the passage of time. Tarot cards are another tool used with candle spells, being placed in front or behind for added visual intent.

Another popular magical approach is to drop a stone or gem into the candle spell as it is burning, so that the stone is covered in the melting wax, releasing more energy into the spell, or placing stones or crystals around the candle for the balance of additional energy influences. Clear crystal may be used to enhance the energy, while the qualities of stones, taken from your BOS listing, may be used to enhance the particular purpose of the spell. Red jasper may be added to the candle for protection, jet to bind the spell, and so forth.

Once the spell is complete, you can remove the stone that was dropped into the candle, and rub off the wax residue before washing it in cold running water (in a sink is fine). Do a quick cleansing for stones and crystals after their use in spell work by rinsing them off in water, then passing them through the symbols of the Elementals. Having a flat piece of amethyst to set the stone or crystal on overnight will help to refresh it, but otherwise, wrap it in black cloth and put it away.

Elixirs may be used as a wash for a ritual or spell object, or may be drunk as an internal energy enhancer. The listing in chapter two shows some connections of stone and energy for elixirs. All that is needed to create this drink is spring water and the stone, placed in the water under the light of the Full Moon, and then stored, perhaps with a drop of an alcohol such as vodka, whiskey, rum, or gin as a preservative. If you abstain from alcohol, do not use this method of preservation, but instead simply keep the elixir tightly bottled and stored in a cool, dark place.

Working with Herbs

Herbs are an integral part of Green Witchcraft, being used as additives in spells, planted in the yard, or potted around the home for protective and nurturing influences, and used in crafts, pillows, sachets, oils, and magical cooking. When you are attuned to the powers around you, every aspect of your life becomes infused with magic, and this shows in everything from cooking and cleaning to crafting and gardening. There are many books available on herb gardening, and if you want to work with herbs, you should look into some of these, adjusting as needed for your particular geographical area.

Although many herbs like full sun, if you live in a desert area or a place where the sun burns very hot, then you will find that the herbs will do better when protected by the partial shading of a tree. The soil condition optimal for herbs varies by the plant, as does the life-span. Some herbs like a rich soil, others are content with a sandy ground, so you need to plant your garden to accommodate the plants. Watering will also vary, with some liking a moist soil, and others preferring near dry conditions. I have found that those herbs that are not comfortable in the herb beds do very well in their own planter boxes, as long as these have sufficient growing space. To keep the herbs producing leaves, nip off the buds before they flower, and trim them back. I have kept one marjoram plant for five years this way, when most people consider these to be annuals rather than perennials. My rosemary is nearly ten years old now, and is a good size shrub, dominating the entrance to the beds, so you can nurture your herbs through the years. Consider also the personalities of the plants you are tending. Some are suited to the community bed, while others prefer the privacy of their own planter. If you have an herb that is not thriving in the garden bed, try transplanting it into a large planter and see how it fares. With something like wood Betony, pennyroyal, or St. Johnswort, the planter may be preferred since these herbs will spread quickly. The wood betony is especially prone to taking over an herb garden, with plants sprouting all along its roving roots, permeating every corner of the bed.

Herbs are often considered weeds, so they are pretty hardy little folk. You can prepare your beds for winter by trimming them down, then covering them with straw or burlap for the season. I have tarragon that comes back with enthusiasm every year after the winter trimming. Another point to consider is the manner of growth for your plants. Ginger can be cut down every year, the roots dug up, separated, and stored in a cool, dry place for the winter, then planted in spring. Root plants are easy to care for, increasing their population every season, and you have the advantage of placing them where you most want them.

Elder trees are another plant that multiplies for you much the same as the wood betony, only elders put out shoots from their roots that develop into little trees close around the base of the tree trunk. Once the new plant is eight to twelve inches tall, you can remove the youngster from Mama and transplant this sapling to another area of the yard. If the shock of moving causes all the leaves to fall off, do not despair. This is rather like weaning a baby from mother's milk, for up until now, the sapling has drawn sustenance from the roots of the mother tree. Within a week, the young tree will sprout new leaves to become self-sufficient. Always talk to the mother tree and her child before you begin moving the sapling so that they understand what you are doing. The young tree will be healthier and grow bigger if not kept under mother's shadow, and in time, will send up offspring of its own. You can also root a sapling by setting it in a vase of water for a few days, then planting it once the roots start to appear.

To gather the herbs for your magical use, always tell the plant what you need and wait to see what response you can sense. Sometimes the plant will generate an image to you that tells you which leaf or flower is best for your purpose. When I had once lost my grip on a hot iron, pushing it against my thumb, I rushed out to the herb garden and drew a pentagram before the comfrey plant as I asked the herb for a leaf to put on the burn. Immediately several leaves offered themselves—many more than I needed, and so I took one and blessed the plant for its generosity. I wrapped the leaf around an ice cube and pressed it against my thumb, and a blister never developed. In looking back at the incident, I remember how gentle and caring the plant felt to me, the energies of concern and willingness to help coming to me in waves. The plant offered me its most tender, bright green leaves, but as with all things of Nature, we only take what we need, nothing more, and with appreciation and respect for the energies. Part of being connected is being open to these emanations and sensations, allowing the intuitive mind to function.

Remember that with the Green Craft, the rule is that you must give a gift to get a gift, so when you gather an herb for spell work, offer the plant a blessing, inscribe a sigil of health in the soil at the base of the plant, or pour a bit of milk on the ground before it. Other gifts could be a design of a pentagram, drawing a protection circle around the plant, pressing a penny into the ground, leaving crushed eggshells around it, or pouring a libation of spring water at the roots.

Sigils are another versatile tool that may be used as part of the process of spell crafting. They are composed of one, two, or three runic symbols that are combined, with the last one being the binding one. You can create any sigil by associating the runic meanings with your goal, and as you draw the last rune, state what it is, the meaning, and add the words, "(rune) for (intent) and to bind them all."

Timing is important for herb gathering as well. For the best results, besides following the Moon symbology for the spell work, you can collect herbs according to the intent you have for their use. If inaugurating a new project, pick your herbs when the Moon is waxing, moving from dark to full. This is also a good time for spells that bring gains to you, so you would want to collect those types of herbs according to the correlations in your BOS. To store energy, collect your herbs when the Moon is waning, moving from full to dark. This is also a good time for spells that rid you of things such as illness or a bad habit, so you would want to collect herbs at this time for this type of purpose. You can also include the influence of astrological signs when you collect plants, looking at the association of that time and ruling planet.

Planting your garden may also be conducted in rhythm with the lunar influences. Plant flowering annuals and above ground plants that have seeds (such as wheat or oats) between the dark and first quarter of the Moon. Between the first quarter and the full phase, you can plant those above-ground plants that have internally contained seeds (such as peas). Between the full and last quarter phases, you can plant root crops, bulbs, and perennials (such as herbs), while between the last quarter and the dark phase of the Moon, you should not plant anything.

Collecting herbs is best done in the early morning on a dry day. The general rule is that once you have gathered an herb, it should not touch the ground lest the energy conserved within drain away into the Earth for rebirth. You might want to use a basket to put your cuttings in as you trim them from the main plant. If the gathered plant does end up on the ground, see it as in touch with the Earth energies from which it sprang and call upon these energies to revitalize the plant.

Mugwort should be gathered before the flowers open, as is pretty much the case for all herbs, rosemary being a notable exception. Dry the herbs in a cool dark place, then crumble the leaves from the stems and store the leaves in glass jars, keeping them away from direct sunlight (which can fade them). Most herbs can be tied in bundles of two or three stems and hung by a string indoors, or they may be tied together and hung with the flowers hanging down (as with calendula). It only takes three to seven days for the herbs to be ready for mincing, grinding, or storing as whole leaves. Always label your jars for quick recognition, that way you won't have to keep opening the lids to sniff the contents for clues as to what is in the container.

A number of herb crafts can be a part of spell crafting, including making herbal wreaths. A mugwort circle is very easy to make since the herb is flexible and can be looped together, retaining its shape. This is a simple charm for protection and psychic opening, and the loop can be placed on top of your crystal ball, or hung over the door of your magic room. Wreaths and swaths may be made and placed around the house where they can exert their beneficial influences. Fennel can be placed over doors and windows to invoke the protection of the God, while rosemary brings the blessing of the Goddess. Willow and grapevine bend easily and make excellent bases for any herbal, cloth, fruit, or greenery wreath you may want to construct. Other images may be created with willow and vine, from stars to balls, and you can place herbal decorations on these or tuck a fragrant sachet or clove-studded orange pomander inside.

Filling dream pillows with herbs is another craft that invokes the energies of the plants—these may be used in dream work when placed under the sleeper's pillow, and also used for protection when placed in a car. There are many ways to use a dream pillow, which is really a type of herbal sachet used with magical intent rather than simply to provide fragrance in your linens drawer. The herbal content determines the influence being attracted. A fairy dream pillow may be created and hung in a tree to honor and invoke the blessings of the Other People, or a prosperity pillow can be made and tucked away inside a purse. Essential oils may be added to enhance the fragrance, and a little batting (used to stuff quilts, and often found in the material and sewing sections of stores) softens the texture of the pillow.

Making Magical Herb Teas

Another popular method of gaining benefits from magical herbs is through making and drinking teas. Along with magical benefits, a number of medical benefits can be derived from herbal teas. There are many books that cover these medicinal uses quite well, but I have mainly focused on the magical applications. As with all herbal use, self-discipline is a must. Periodically there are news articles decrying the dangers of herbal usage, and demands for Federal control over herbs, generally from the American Medical Association (AMA) or the Food and Drug Administration (FDA). One major reason for this problem is that people can and do develop serious health problems, particularly organ damage and system breakdowns, simply because they overdose themselves.

Comfrey tea is a prime example of how a weak tea intended to soothe irritable bowls or ulcers, and meant for minimal consumption of one cup a day for no more than one or two days, has been defined as a menace to humanity because after ingesting large quantities, people develop liver failure or liver cancer. Basically, comfrey, which has the property of stimulating new cell growth, is an external medicine meant to treat skin irritations (like my burned thumb) and insect bites as a salve, and many herbalists do not recommend ingesting this herb at all. St. Johnswort has become popular as a mood enhancer and to ease depression, but extensive use of this herb makes the skin sensitive to sunlight.

Echineachea is not intended to be used as a daily dose like a vitamin pill, either. You take a double dose once on the day you feel a cold or flu coming on, then a single dose no more than three times a day for the next two or three days, and that is all your immune system needs to kick into gear. As for dieting teas, if the main ingredient is cascara sagrada or senna, you are drinking a laxative. These herbs were intended as a one-time dose to treat constipation. If you keep drinking it, you will flush out of your system a number of vital chemicals, such as potassium, and may even induce irregular heartbeat, hives, and vomiting. Other major ingredients in diet teas may simply be massive doses of caffeine, promoted as an aid to speed up metabolism, but which may cause irregular heart beat and high blood pressure. The reality is that any tea will act as a natural diuretic, flushing excess water from your cells.

A tea made of cassias augustifolias should be a one-time dose only, and depending on your system, may need to be followed up the next day with plain black tea to counteract a reaction of diarrhea. This herb is used to stimulate a menstrual cycle and to counteract constipation. I cannot imagine anyone taking this type of tea for the length of time required for dieting without becoming extremely debilitated. The side-effects of diarrhea associated with these teas include loss of needed chemicals, vitamins, and minerals to dehydration and loss of electrolytes. Young children can die from extended diarrhea, while stronger adults tend to develop strange ailments, from skin disease to organ failure. Alfalfa can lead to miscarriage and disorders in a person's autoimmune system, while an overdose of rue and pennyroyal can be fatal, cause spontaneous abortion, or lead to liver damage. With all herbal use, remember that herbs were taken as medication from ancient times and need to be treated with respect and caution.

The teas given here are intended to be used as one cup in conjunction with working magic. If you are pregnant or think you might be, or if you have allergies, you need to be particularly careful, and perhaps even avoid ingesting some varieties of herbal tea in your magic practice. You could instead use the tea as a wash for magical supplies, as with washing a crystal ball with cooled mugwort tea to enhance divination, or as an additive to other washings, such as for floors, laundry (adding lavender to the machine when washing ritual clothing and altar cloths, as an example), and altars. For more information on the medicinal cautions for herbs, you may want to consult an herb book such as *Earl Mendell's Herb Bible*, by Earl Mendell, R.Ph, Ph.D. (Simon & Schuster, New York, 1992).

I have used herbal teas for many years, but with respect for the powers of the herbs, both magical and medicinal. In making tea, I like to place the herbs in a china teapot along with black tea leaves (either loose or in tea bags). If you are not doing tea leaf readings, you could place the herbs and tea leaves in a tea ball, cloth tea bag (these are commercially sold and come with a drawstring closing) or strainer that fits in the teapot. If you are doing tea leaf readings, you will want to use loose tea in the pot so that when you pour the tea, some of the leaves will go into the cup. If using loose tea in the pot, and you are not planning on doing readings with the leaves, you can also use a hand-held strainer as you pour the tea into the cup. The teapot is placed on the stove next to the burner where cold water is brought to a boil in a tea kettle, so as to warm the teapot, or you could swirl a little hot water in the teapot and pour it out before adding the black tea, herbs, and the boiling water. Cover the pot with a tea cozy or towel while the tea steeps for three to five minutes. The longer tea sits, the stronger it becomes, and after half an hour to forty-five minutes you should not be drinking it as it will be very acidic.

The purpose of drinking a magical tea is to bring the mind into focus on the magical work about to be started. The energies of the herbs are called upon as the herbs are being dropped into the pot, so that you are stating the name of the herb and the association you are making with that herb. A magical tea is a potion, with a magical intent, and you relate the ingredients to that intent, which you derive from the herbal correspondence listing in your BOS.

For divination tea, put into the teapot a teaspoon each of mugwort leaves, lemon balm, rose hips, and a tea bag of any black tea (English Teatime, Irish or English Breakfast, etc.), saying:

> *I call upon thee, mugwort, to aid in my divinations;*
> *I call upon thee, lemon balm, to bring success in my*
>   *divinations;*
> *I call upon thee, rose hips, to aid my psychic power in my*
>   *divinations;*
> *I call upon thee black tea to boost the power of this potion.*

You can have the person who is receiving the reading concentrate on a particular question when holding their teacup. Have the person drink almost all of the tea, leaving a residue of tea leaves in a bit of liquid. Traditionally, the person then swishes the tea around in a circle, overturns the cup onto the saucer with the cup handle toward them, and turns the upside-down cup three times before handing it over to the reader. I have done readings like this, but the ceremony is really just mood setting, and a good reading can be effected simply by swishing the tea leaves three times clockwise around the cup with the bit of liquid, and looking at the symbols within. You may want to add a chant of your own creation, but my favorite is:

Swirl the leaves and set the tea;
Clear and true this reading see;
Lord and Lady stand by me;
Guide my sight, So Mote It Be!

The handle is the starting point, with events moving clockwise around the cup. If you are reading for a day, week, month, or year, you state so before the tea is swirled, and the handle is the starting point for you to subdivide into hours, days, or months.

Drinking a soothing cup of tea prior to your workings can aid in both your divination and spell work. It helps to set the mood and relaxes the mind so that you are ready to enter into the magical altered state quickly. It is a good practice to keep a large stock of herbs and teas in the cupboard (away from the light) for creating your own tea combinations. A base of black tea for power wards negativity while adding strength and flavor to the herbal tea blends, and the combinations can be quite delicious. By blending your own teas you can draw upon the powers of the herbs toward a particular goal. The many combinations are also beneficial in drawing the natural energies of the devas into your own sphere and infusing yourself with their magical properties to aid in your workings.

Divination teas can also include a teaspoon of eyebright for sight, while elderflower, fennel, and hops may be used for health spells. Rose hips, damiana, and chamomile are additives for love spells, but by substituting elderflower for the rose hips, you have a meditation tea. A tea for purification can include the versatile chamomile, along with fennel seed, hyssop leaves, and valerian. For a wash of protection, you could combine burdock root, comfrey, elderflower, hyssop, linden (tila), rose hips, and valerian. Other tea ingredients you can use according to their properties in your BOS listing are bergamot, black cohosh, calendula (marigold flower), chickweed, dandelion root, fenugreek, feverfew, goldenseal, hops, Irish moss, lemon balm, mint, mugwort, mullein, nettle, orange peel, parsley, raspberry leaf, rosemary, skullcap, slippery elm bark, spearmint, thyme, uva ursi, valerian root, white oak bark, wild cherry bark, and yarrow.

You can also make a simmering potpourri of various herbs as part of your spell work, using herbs suited to drawing money, love, or simply creating a special atmosphere through scent. With a potpourri for money, you can chant as the steam fills the air:

> *Let this spell be spread into the air;*
> *Grant that nothing may my work impair;*
> *Bring success and wealth to me;*
> *As this I spell and as I will, So Mote It Be!*

Today, scent disbursal is an aspect of aromatherapy, but Witches have been using the fragrance of herbs for magical workings for centuries. Herbs have also been used as additives to baths for thousands of years, with this infusion being absorbed by the body as well as generating magical influences through scent. Add incense and candlelight, and you are wrapped in magical energies, perfect for releasing negativity and preparing for spell work. Check your herbal listing for the qualities you seek to add to your bath water: calendula, chamomile, dianthus, heather, jasmine, lavender, lemon balm, marjoram, rose, rosemary, savory, thyme, and so forth.

Magical Herbal Oils

Herbs have been traditionally used in the Craft for creating oils for candle dressing, consecrations, anointings at the start of ritual, and cleansings. Oils are also used to revitalize and refresh an area, purging it of any negativity that may have built up, perhaps as an additive to spring water. Herbs may be ground up and combined in a bottle with an oil such as mineral, olive, sunflower, or safflower, and allowed to steep for a period of time. When you have the desired aroma, shake the bottle, then strain it through cheesecloth into a clean bottle for storage away from direct sunlight, and use as desired. You may steep the ground herbs in spring water, adding a touch of essential oil as well. When applying the oil to yourself for ritual, you may want to draw a symbol on your forehead such as a solar cross in a circle, a solar cross and lunar spiral, or a pentagram. For other magical purposes, such as enhancing astral projection, you can also apply the oil to pulse points at the temples, wrists, inner elbows, back of the knees, ankles, and the soles of the feet. There are a number of books available on the various techniques and uses for oils and ointments created for magical purposes, and you may want to augment your library with one or two of these.

Talisman and Amulet Magic

A talisman is something that you make and carry with you or wear for protection or to attract a particular energy. A crystal, gem, or stone may be made into a talisman by inscribing or painting it with a sigil that represents your intention, be it protection, safe travel, or business success. It is then carried or placed where you want it to have the best effect. You should re-invigorate the talisman periodically by passing it through the symbols of the Elementals during an Esbat celebration. Talismans may also be constructed out of metals with a pertinent design created to designate the focus of the piece, and thus most are familiar to us as religious jewelry, from medals and crosses on a chain to runic symbols and pentacles on a cord or ring. The word itself is derived from the Greek word for religious rites, and so the implication is that the talisman has spiritual connotations. Nevertheless, the talisman has been adapted to service in other energy fields over the years, drawing positive forces to the holder in the various aspects of the person's life, be it spiritual, personal, or career oriented.

An amulet is usually a natural item that attracts energies, such as carrying a four-leaf clover for good luck, particularly when engaging in some activity of fortune such as playing games and buying lottery tickets. The effectiveness of the amulet is related to the energy of the object. A belief in the power of a rabbit's foot or a chicken's foot to attract magical energies makes them standard amulets among some magical groups. Roots such as the mandrake, feathers, and acorns are other examples of items from Nature carried for good fortune and protection. Crystals and gems may figure as amulets as well, but usually these are a part of jewelry worn as mundane adornment. Amulets are not intended as adornment but are worn or carried for their energy properties.

Both amulets and talismans may be charged according to your intent. If you see the object as attracting success, as attracting good luck, then you will want to use the Waxing to Full Moon. But if you intend the object to deflect, repel, or return-to-sender negative energies, you will want to charge it by the Waning to Dark Moon.

Working Magic for Others

Spells are generally done on a personal basis for the advantage of the Witch. However, there are times when other people will approach a Practitioner of the Craft for assistance in attaining a particular goal. The ideal is that the Witch who conducts magic for someone receives a token gift or service in payment, but the reality is that spell materials may cost money in one way or another, and money is often used today, since labor or barter goods are somewhat out of fashion in our far-flung society. People advertise spell work in catalogs and magazines, and if the people doing the magic are competent, there really is nothing wrong with this. The main idea of giving a gift to receive a gift may be adapted to monetary payments if this is the most convenient for the person seeking the service. But when it comes to important matters, there are certain dangers involved with working spells for other people. One of the primary difficulties is that a person must sincerely want the spell done.

I have learned through experience that people will say one thing and think another, which of course derails a spell and can even throw it into a different direction. You are moving energy, with the cooperation and assistance of another person, and just as with coven work, you must both be on the same energy page for this to work. The result of asking for one thing, but of mentally attaching conditions, is that once those conditions are met, the spell will work, but not necessarily as the person originally wanted. In addition to this problem, you also have to know the facts in a matter. It is not unusual for someone to say they want one thing, but are actually looking at a different situation. Most of all, you need to preserve yourself from unwanted Karma by application of your ethical standard. If the person who comes to you for spell casting does not feel a need to abide by the Rede or the Rules, then you should not perform the magic on their behalf. Sometimes a more oblique magical working will suffice and you may want to confer with the individual and discuss alternatives rather than simply rejecting the request for help. In many ways, Witches are counselors and mediators, and so many are drawn to the field of psychology to be better equipped to help others understand their true motivations for turning to another for assistance in a matter. It does no good to cast a spell for someone if that person simply repeats the same errors because the cause of a situation, for example, is not being addressed. Some people repeat Karmic lessons because they do not take the time to learn from their mistakes.

The bottom line in doing magic for others is your comfort level. If you feel pressured, that may be a detriment, but if you feel sincerely for someone's situation, you can always do your spell work in a manner that places the raised energy into the loving hands of the Lady and the Lord for manifestation. Again, Perfect Love and Perfect Trust are important factors in your personal practice of magic. I was once accosted by a woman who was very insistent that I do a candle spell for her. She was living in a shelter with her two young children, and although she had approached a number of other people at a Pagan gathering to give her magical assistance, she became obsessed with staying close to me and glaring at me. Whether or not she knew that she was directing negative energies to me was not the issue, and I had no trouble deflecting the energies. What mattered to me was the situation with her innocent children, who came there quiet and withdrawn, but responded positively to any attention offered them over the next few hours, so that by the end of the evening, they were laughing and playing. In her case, there was no payment, or even a consideration of payment, but the need of her children surpassed hers. The Fairies love children, and it was through the Fair Ones, with the children in mind, that I could comfortably light a candle for the woman. Here the thought was that what is good for the children will be drawn to them through their mother, but the whole of the matter was directed through the Fair Ones and through the love of the Goddess and the God.

If you enjoy working magic for others, such as for encouraging pregnancy or cleansing a house, for example, then you should receive at least some kind of token payment, be it food, an art or craft item, or money. My grandmother used to receive gifts of various sorts including labor around the yard and even live chickens. The idea of binding the energy of the spell is what matters. But if you are not comfortable with working for others, you can help them through instruction to help themselves, or refer them to someone you know who might be better prepared to assist them.

Following Your Own Path

There are any number of spells that you can construct using the basic information and correlations presented in this work. Once you determine which of the correspondences suits your needs, and have worked through one or two spells on your own, you will develop a feel for how it all comes together. The samples found in spell books should act as a guide for you, not as the end-all of spell crafting. Each person adds a little of their own personality into a spell and that is what makes it relevant and workable. In all things, when you are uncertain or have questions and need direction, you have only to ask the Lady and the Lord for guidance and they will help you.

The main concern for timing spells in the Green Path relates to the position of the Moon for the enhancement of energy raising. The Waxing Moon is used for growth and new projects, the Full Moon for healing and empowerment, the Waning Moon for releasing, banishing, and cleansing, and the Dark or New Moon for divination. But if you need a spell *now*, and the Moon is in a waning phase, all you have to do is think in reverse terms, so that, as an example, instead of drawing good health, work magic to banish ill health or to cleanse yourself of the ailment. Instead of drawing money, think of releasing poverty. Instead of drawing love, think of banishing loneliness. All these are ways to work toward a positive goal by ridding yourself of the negative opposite. Magic is a craft, a skill, and an art, and creativity in outlook will help you to be more flexible in your workings. If you want to be rid of something and the phase is for gaining, seek to gain that which will by the gaining eliminate what you wish to cast away.

It is not enough to read or to listen to lectures about conducting magic, you must perform the magic yourself to gain proficiency. Meditation, visualization, and seeing the associations of everyday objects as Earth, Air, Fire, and Water influenced or aligned will help organize your thought patterns. Have reasons for your associations, tune into your own feelings about herbs and other beings of Nature, and understand your motivations, ensuring that they fall within the ethical guidelines of your Craft. By opening your intuition to the secrets of the Earth spirits, you will discover new correlations and amend the listings you work with, and through further research, you will discover that you are not alone in this. Your practice will always be developing and growing, for that is the powerful impetus of Nature, and we are always learning. Through continuing your magic practice, you will find that your skill will evolve so that you will work with perfect love and perfect trust in the guidance of the Divine.

Appendix A

CORRESPONDENCES FOR A BOOK OF SHADOWS

Herbal/Plant Correspondences by Name and Use

Acacia—altar offering/consecration, aids psychic powers, meditation

Agrimony—protection, returns spells to their sender, promotes sleep

Alder—whistles entice the Elemental Air, Fairy invocations

Allspice—prosperity, energy

Angelica—protection, divination, consecration

Anise—purify/consecrate, protection, spirit aid in spells, divination, aids creativity

Apple—food for departing spirits, love, health, attract unicorns

Ash—wands, protection, leaves for prophetic dreams, prosperity

Avens—purification, love, protection from negative energies

Banana (leaf/flower)—fertility, prosperity, Goddess and God as One Divinity

Basil—protection, courage, wealth, love, divination, creativity, repels negativity

Bay—psychic powers, purification, wishes, divination, justice, wisdom, promotion

Benzoin—purification, prosperity, meditation

Bergamot—success, wealth, justice

Betony—purification, protection, psychic awareness, banish despair/nightmares

Birch—wands, protection, purification, ward negativity, cleansing

Blackberry—protection, health, prosperity, Shadowland

Blackthorn—return evil to the sender, thwart negative energies, barrier

Borage—psychic power, protection, courage

Briar—clairvoyant dreams, Fairy magics

Broom—purification, protection, non-Fairy magics only as they do not like it

Burdock—ward negativity, purification, protection

Cardamom—love, romance

Carnation (Dianthus)—protection, strength, healing, Goddess offering

Catnip—love, creativity, cat magics, familiars, restfulness

Chamomile—meditation, rest, purification, calmness, prosperity

Cherry—creativity, hope, expectations

Cinnamon—spiritual/psychic powers, protection, success, business, healing

Cinquefoil—prosperity, protection, purification, divination, healing, good fortune

Citron—psychic ability, clarity

Clove—wealth, purification, ward negativity, cleansing

Clover—divination, consecrations, money, luck, love, Otherworld

Coltsfoot—karma, political power

Comfrey—healing, safe travel

Coriander—health, money

Cornflower—psychic ability

Cumin—protection of belongings

Damiana—divination, protection of property

Dill—money, protection, love

Dittany of Crete—divination, psychic power

Dragon's Blood—consecration, power, life cycle, changes

Elder—wands, Fairies, blessings (never burn the wood), magic power

Elm—Elves, love

Eyebright—aiding mental powers, divination

Fennel—protection, sacred to the God, deflect negative energies

Ferns—protection, calling rain, wisdom

Feverfew—ward sickness, ward accidents in travel

Fir—manifestation

Foxglove [POISON]—grown to protect the house and yard, source of digitalis

Frankincense—protection, blessing, spirituality, meditation, power

Furze/Gorse—protection, preparation for conflict

Garlic—protection, power

Ginger—love, success, money, power

Hawthorn—wands, fertility, protection, creativity/Witchery skills, Fairy attraction

Hazel—Fairies, healing, protection, luck, communication, wands

Heather—(red) love, (white) protection, (purple) spiritual development, beauty

Holly—balance, dream magic

Honeysuckle—divination, dreams

Hops—health, sleep, divination

Hyssop—purification, wards negativity

Iris—wisdom

Ivy—protection, friendship, healing, perseverance

Kelp—winds, protection, psychic powers

Lavender—Elves, purification, peace, psychic awareness, creativity, cleansing

Lemon balm—success, health, love, justice, good luck

Lilac—protection, Underworld, Otherworld, beauty, love

Linden—(lime tree) protection, immortality, good fortune, sleep, love

Loosestrife—harmony, peace, accord

Mace—psychic power, alertness

Marigold—marriage, clairvoyant dreams, Fairies, protection, psychic powers

Marjoram—love, protection, wealth

Mint—protection, prosperity, offering to helpful spirits

Mistletoe [POISON]—fertility, consecration, protection, healing, psychic ability

Motherwort—protection, confidence, wards negative energies, imagination

Moonwort—divination, love, prosperity

Mugwort—divination, consecration, strength, protection

Mullein—protection, purification, divination, health, courage

Mustard—good luck, health, protection, fertility

Myrrh—protection, ward negativity, purification/consecration, Underworld, binding

Nettle—Elves, Fairies, consecration, restore balance, protection, life cycles

Nutmeg—prosperity, comfort

Nuts and Cones—fertility, drawing wealth

Oak—wands, purification, money, health

Oats—wealth, security, offering

Orange Peel—love, good fortune, divination

Orris Root—companionship, spirit communication, protection, occultism, divination

Parsley—purification, protection

Patchouli—money, fertility, Earth, Underworld

Pecan—prosperity, abundance

Pepper—protection, ward negativity

Pine—purification, cleansing, money, courage

Rose (hips)—love, divination, psychic power

Rosemary—purification, blessing, protection, love, health, Elves, courage

Rowan—wands, knowledge, divination, spirit help, home protection, inspiration

Rue [POISON]—blessing, consecration, protection, health, ward negative energy

Sage—protection, wisdom, health, purification, artistic ability

St. Johnswort—good health, willpower, enhance creativity, banish negativity

Sandalwood—protection, ward negativity, spirit offering

Solomon's Seal (Dropberry; Sealroot)—Elemental offering, protection

Star Anise—psychic power, good fortune

Straw—Fairies, images, protection *(do not burn magic infused straw)*

Sunflower—Elves, purification, consecrations, changes, bright prospects

Tansy—health, happiness

Thyme—ward negativity, courage, purification, healing, psychic power, swift action

Trefoil—Fairies, protection, luck

Vervain—offering, love, purification, riches, creativity, visions, ward psychic attack

Vetivert—love, money, ward negativity

Wheat—fertility, wealth, good fortune

Willow—wands, divination, love, protection

Woodruff—clear away barriers, protection, success, changes, psychic awareness

Wormwood (Absinthe) [POISON]—evocation, divination/scrying, protection

Yarrow—divination, love, happy marriage, ward negativity, defense, protection

Yew [POISON]—death and rebirth, athame handle

Dark Power Herbal/Plant Associations

Absinthe—Crone, Dark Moon, Lunar Eclipse, Underworld

Acacia—inspiration, protection, Lughnassadh passage, psychic power

Agrimony—exorcism, sleep, calming, protection, return-to-sender

Amaranth (cockscomb)—passages, Samhain, immortality, spirit communication

Anise—Crone, protection, purification, psychic power, divination, seeking answers, spirit contact, deflection of negativity

Apple—Underworld, rebirth, immortality, food for the dead, Samhain

Artemesia—Dark Lady, Dark Moon, Lunar Eclipse

Asafetida—a bad-smelling resin used for exorcism and protection

Ash (bark/leaves)—death, passage, Beltane, protection, health, prophecy, insight, dreams

Avens—exorcism, purification

Balsam—Underworld passage, psychic energy, spirit communication

Bay—Yule, Imbolc, psychic power, strength, purification, healing

Bayberry—Yule, transition

Belladonna (Deadly Nightshade) [POISON—substitute Dittany of Crete or Mugwort]—Samhain, astral travel, psychic power, visions

Blackberry—Dark Lord, Lughnassadh, Hunter, protection

Black Currant (cassias)—Lord of Shadows, Hunter/Crone, Wild Hunt, Shadowland

Blackthorn—defense, deflect negativity, retribution, protection, Otherworld contact

Boneset—deflection, exorcism, protection

Briar—defense, protection, enhance witch's power, divination, dreams

Burdock—wards negativity, purification, protection

Clove—banishing/releasing, exorcism, protection, spirit companion offering

Cypress—banishing/releasing, binding, death, immortality, eternity, Underworld, Shadowland, Hades, Hecate, Cybele, oracles

Damiana—visions, healing

Dandelion (root)—psychic power, spirit contact, Otherworld

Dianthus (carnation)—protection, power, health, blood, regeneration

Dittany of Crete—astral travel, spirit communication

Dragon's Blood (palm resin)—binding, changes, courage, energy, strength, power, exorcism, protection

Elder—Crone, banishing/releasing, defense, deflection, retribution, Litha, blessings, wards negativity, Otherworld, protection, visions, spirit contact, occult learning, healing, exorcism

Elecampagne (elfdock)—psychic power, protection, divination, Otherworld contact

Elm (elvin)—protection, attraction, energy, passages

Fennel—protection, purification, healing, ward negativity

Fern—banishing/releasing, exorcism, protection, Samhain, Otherworld

Fir—Yule, Underworld, arcane wisdom

Foxglove [POISON; substitute Tamarisk]—defense, protection, return to sender, deflection

Frankincense—anointing, strength, power, energy, exorcism, Yule, Beltane, Lughnassadh, protection, consecration, visions

Garlic—protection, ward negativity, invoke the Dark Goddess, exorcism, healing

Ginger (root)—psychic power, protection, exorcism, deflection, return to sender, drawing, spirit contact

Gorse (furze)—protection, preparation for conflict

Hawthorn—protection, Witchcraft power, Otherworld, Beltane, ward negativity, attract Fairies

Hazel—invoke Otherworld aid, attract Fair Folk, enhance Witch's power

Hellebore [POISON; substitute Black Currant]—Crone, Lord of Shadows, visions, Underworld, psychic power, exorcism, astral travel

Hemlock [POISON; substitute Lilac]—power, purification, protection, astral travel

Henbane [POISON; substitute Mace]—Underworld, spirit contact

Holly [POISON; substitute Frankincense]—energy, strength, power, insight, protection, deflection

Hyssop—protection, purification, cleansing, remove negativity/malevolence

Jasmine—anointing, balance, Ostara, divination, dreams, insight, astral projection

Jimsonweed (datura) [POISON; substitute Agrimony]—deflection, return to sender, ward negativity, protection

Juniper Berry—visions, purification, spirit contact, exorcism, protection

Lady's Slipper—ward negative energy, return to sender, protection, deflection

Lavender (elf leaf)—anointing, exorcism, purification, Litha, honor Ancient Ones, protection, cleansing, Otherworld/Sidhe contact, opening psychic centers, spirit contact

Lilac—Underworld, Beltane, exorcism, protection, cleansing

Linden—immortality, protection, Underworld

Mace—psychic power, enhance spirit contact, Underworld

Mandrake [POISON; substitute Ginger Root or Fennel Root]—calling upon spirits, communicate with spirits, offering, exorcism, protective watcher

Marigold (Calendula)—divination, Otherworld, Fairy offering, Beltane, Mabon, protection, dreams, psychic power

Mastic—spirit contact, enhance psychic power, strength

May-apple (American Mandrake) [POISON; substitute Ginger Root or Fennel Root]—spirit contact, death, spirit offering, substitute for mandrake

Mugwort (artemesia)—Dark Lady, Dark Moon, Lunar Eclipse, psychic power, dreams, banishing/releasing, divination, cleansing magic mirrors and crystal balls, Litha, astral projection, strength, protection, healing

Mullein—Crone energy, courage, exorcism, graveyard dust, divination, protection, return to sender, deflection

Myrrh—Imbolc, Mabon, exorcism, protection, purification, power

Nettle—protection, exorcism, return to sender, deflection, courage

Nightshade (Bittersweet) [POISON; substitute Mugwort]—Crone/Hunter energy, return to sender, Lunar Eclipse, Solar Eclipse, banishing/releasing, astral projection, strength

Oak (galls/leaves/wood/acorns)—strength, power, purification, charms, wisdom, truth, Litha, Mabon, Samhain, Yule

Orris Root—power, protection, divination, deflection

Paprika—protection, wards malevolent energy, deflection

Patchouli—Samhain, Underworld, passage, Earth energies

Pennyroyal [POISON; substitute Blackthorn]—deflection, power, protection, ward negative energy

Peppercorn—protection, power, deflection, exorcism

Pomegranate—Underworld, passage, hidden wealth, attainment, protection, deflection, secret knowledge

Purple Heather—peace, cleansing, spiritual attainment, Samhain, Imbolc, Lughnassadh

Rosemary (elf leaf)—courage, exorcism, protection, purification, dreams, health, strength, cleansing, Otherworld, Sidhe contact

Rowan (Mountain Ash)—binding, divination, secret knowledge, divination, calling upon spirits, calling upon the Sidhe for aid, psychic power, protection, Underworld travels

Rue [POISON; substitute Tamarisk]—exorcism, health, enhance magics, return to sender, deflection, retribution, ward malevolence/negative energies

Sage—Yule, Mabon, immortality, wisdom, protection, spirit/Otherworld offering, exorcism, purification

Sandalwood—meditation, intuitive power, protection, spirit contact, exorcism

Skullcap—protection, healing, passage to Underworld

St. Johnswort—banishing/releasing, Otherworld, Midsummer (Litha), power, protection

Tamarisk (Flowering Cypress)—exorcism, divination, deflection, return to sender

Tansy—Dark Goddess, immortality, Otherworld offering

Thistle—protection, warding/changing bad luck, Mabon, exorcism, deflection of negative energies, return to sender, spirit contact

Thyme—ward negativity, Litha, protection, psychic power, healing, purification, Otherworld

Turmeric—protection, cleansing, purification

Turnip—Samhain lanterns, spirit lights, ward negative energies, protection, rebirth, passage

Unicorn Root (ague root)—protection, return to sender, exorcism

Valerian—power, purging, releasing, protection, purification

Vervain (Verbena)—purification, cleansing, protection, psychic power, strength, anointing, exorcism, offering, open psychic centers, creativity, Underworld riches, guidance, dreams, divination, Otherworld contact, luck

Vetiver—deflection, ward malevolence, retribution

Willow—Hecate, death, Underworld, passage, protection, spirit contact, deflection

Woodruff—changes, Herne, Greenman, clear barriers, overcome obstacles, Beltane, protection

Wormwood [POISON; substitute Mugwort or Cypress]—binding, divination, exorcism, Samhain, divination, spirit evocation, protection, Dark Moon, Lunar Eclipse, dreams, psychic power

Yarrow (Arrowroot)—exorcism, releasing, divination, psychic power, dreams, protection, guidance, courage

Yew [POISON; substitute Sandalwood or Skullcap]—spirit contact, transitions, death/rebirth, Underworld, Yule

Herbal/Plant Listing by Purpose

Balance—basil, chamomile, comfrey, mullein, nettle, woodruff

Blessing—chamomile, dianthus, elder flowers, fennel, mint, oats, rosemary, rue, vervain

Cleansing/Purification—avens, Betony, benzoin, burdock, clove, hyssop, lavender, mullein, parsley, pine, rosemary, thyme, vervain, wormwood, yarrow

Consecration—acacia, anise, basil, clover, dragon's blood, hyssop, lavender, mistletoe, mugwort, nettle, rosemary, rue, sunflower, vervain

Countering Negative Energies—agrimony, avens, fennel,. holly, hyssop, motherwort, rowan, rue, vervain

Courage—basil, Borage, mullein, rosemary, thyme

Creativity—anise seed, basil, catnip, hawthorn, lavender, St. Johnswort, vervain

Divination—anise seed, basil, bay, cinquefoil, clover, damiana, dittany of Crete, eyebright, honeysuckle, hops, lavender, marigold, moonwort, mugwort, mullein, orange peel, rowan, thyme, vervain, woodruff, wormwood, yarrow

Encourage Changes—dragon's blood, linden, purple heather, woodruff

Energy/Power/Strength—cinquefoil, dragon's blood, elder flower, fennel, St. Johnswort, vervain, woodruff

Fortune/Justice—bay, bergamot, cinquefoil, lemon balm, orange peel, star anise, vervain, woodruff

Happiness/Peace—fennel, lavender, loosestrife, rosemary, vervain, yarrow

Healing—cinquefoil, comfrey, coriander, hops, lavender, lemon balm, mullein, mustard, rosemary, rue, sage, St. Johnswort, tansy, thyme

Love—apple, avens, basil, cardamom, catnip, dill flowers, elm, ginger, lavender, lemon balm, linden leaves, marigold, marjoram, moonwort, mustard seed, orange peel, red heather, rosemary, vetivert, willow, yarrow

Meditation—acacia, benzoin, chamomile, frankincense, woodruff

Money—basil, bergamot, chamomile, clove, dill seeds, mint, moonwort, nutmeg, oats, vetivert

Protection/Defense—Betony, birch, burdock, cumin, dianthus, dill leaves, fennel, fern, marjoram, mint, mugwort, mullein, mustard, parsley, rosemary, rue, sage, vervain, white heather, woodruff, wormwood, yarrow

Psychic Awareness—bay, Betony, burdock, cinnamon, elderflower, lavender, mace, marigold, star anise, woodruff

Releasing Negativity—Betony, clove, hyssop, mugwort, rosemary, St. Johnswort, thyme, vervain, vetivert, yarrow

Sealing/Sending Positive Energy—angelica, wormwood

Spirit Contact/Blessings—lilac, purple heather, mint, Solomon's Seal

Strength/Willpower—rosemary, St. Johnswort

Wisdom—elder, sage, willow

Herbal/Plant Listing by Dark Power Purpose

Return-To-Sender [bounce back specifically sent harmful intent and negativity]—agrimony, ginger, lady's slipper, mullein, nettle, rue, tamarisk, thistle, unicorn root

Deflection [diffuse malevolence or ill will] anise, blackthorn, boneset, elder, ginger, lady's slipper, mullein, nettle, orrisroot, paprika, pennyroyal, peppercorn, rue, tamarisk, vetiver, willow

Retribution [return negative energy to sender and seal it there]—blackthorn, elder, rue, vetiver, willow

Curses [call negative energy for a purpose]—cypress, dragon's blood, wormwood, rowan wood, yarrow (arrowroot)

Exorcisms [disperse negative energies so positive energies may enter]—agrimony, asafetida, avens, boneset, clove, cypress, dragon's blood, fern, frankincense, garlic, ginger, juniper berry, lavender, lilac, mullein, nettle, peppercorn, rosemary, rue, sage, sandalwood, tamarisk, thistle, unicorn root, vervain, yarrow (arrowroot)

Purgings and Releasing [lesser exorcisms to absorb negativity for removal]—elder, fern, garlic, hyssop, lavender, lilac, mugwort, onion, sage, skullcap, St. Johnswort, thistle, valerian, willow, woodruff

Crone, Dark Moon, Death-Passages, Hunter, Lunar Eclipse, Otherworld, Protection, Solar Eclipse, Transitions-Rebirth, Underworld—absinthe, acacia, amaranth, anise, apple, ash leaves/berries, artemesia, balsam, bay, bayberry, blackberry, black currant, briar, burdock, cypress, damiana, dandelion root, dianthus, dittany of crete, elder, elecampane, fennel, garlic, ginger root, hawthorn, hazel, jasmine, lavender, lilac, linden, mace, marigold, mugwort, mullein, myrrh, oak, orris root, paprika, patchouli, pomegranate seeds, purple heather, rosemary, rowanwood, sage, sandalwood, skullcap, St. Johnswort, tansy, thistle, thyme, valerian, vervain, willow, woodruff

Appendix A

Herbs/Plants for Sabbat Incense and Decoration

Samhain—burn heather, mullein, patchouli, sage; decorate with acorns, apples, pumpkins, oak leaves, straw, broom, dittany, ferns, flax

Yule—burn bay, bayberry, chamomile, frankincense, rosemary, sage; decorate with holly, juniper, mistletoe, moss, oak, pine cones, cedar, evergreen, blessed thistle

Imbolc—burn basil, bay, benzoin, celandine; decorate with angelica, myrrh, yellow, white, or light blue flowers

Ostara—burn celandine, cinquefoil, jasmine, rose, tansy, violets; decorate with acorn, crocus, daffodil, dogwood, honeysuckle, iris, lily, strawberry

Beltane—burn almond, ash, cinquefoil, frankincense, marigold, meadowsweet, woodruff; decorate with angelica, bluebells, daisy, hawthorn, ivy, lilac, primrose, rose, wildflowers

Litha—burn chamomile, cinquefoil, elder flower, fennel, lavender, mugwort, thyme, vervain; decorate with hemp, larkspur, pine, rose, St. Johnswort, wisteria

Lughnassadh—burn cornstalks, heather, frankincense, wheat; decorate with acacia flowers, corn ears, hollyhock, myrtle, oak leaves, wheat

Mabon—burn benzoin, marigold, myrrh, sage, thistles; decorate with acorns, asters, ferns, honeysuckle, milkweed, mums, oak leaves, pine, rose

Properties of Trees and Shrubs

Alder—water magic, strength, foundations
Apple—love, spirit food, unicorns, beauty, regeneration
Ash—study, health, enhance magic, peace, rebirth, awakening
Aspen—overcoming obstacles, intuition, Otherworld communication
Birch—purification, blessing, health, beginnings, vitality
Blackthorn—control, stimulus, chaos energy

169

Elder—cleansing, offering, Fairies, changes, evolution

Fir/Pine—prosperity, birth/rebirth, power, nobility, discretion, objectivity

Hawthorn—purity, protection, Fairies

Hazel—wisdom, creativity, enhance perceptiveness

Holly—enhances magic, balance, challenges

Ivy—fertility, love, persistence, tenacity

Linden—immortality, protection, good fortune, sleep, love

Mountain Ash (Rowan)—protection, enhances magic, cleansing, insight

Oak—fertility, power, balance, protection, success, truth, strength, courage

Poplar—success, recognition, fame

Vines (grape/berry)—happiness, introspection, renewal, transitions

Willow—Moon magic, psychic power, spirits, death passage, intuition, flexibility

Yew—transformation, psychic awareness, spirits, death passage, immortality

Trees Listed by Daily and Entity Association

Elder/Willow	Monday	Hecate/Crone Goddesses
Holly/Elm/Cedar	Tuesday	Hunter Gods/Elves
Hazel/Rowan	Wednesday	Goddess & God
Oak/Pine	Thursday	The God
Birch/Apple/Myrtle	Friday	The Goddess
Alder/Hawthorn	Saturday	Fairies/Witches
Ash/Birch/Laurel	Sunday	Elves/The Goddess
Ash-Oak-Hawthorn together	Fairie Triad	a haven sacred to the Fair Folk

Elemental Herbal Correspondences

Earth—*material matters; physical form; wealth; career:* balm of Gilead, bistort, cedar, cinquefoil, clove, fern, High John the Conqueror, honeysuckle, horehound, jasmine, mandrake, patchouli, pine, sage, slippery elm

Air—*intellect; mind; creativity; breath; visions; psychic power:* acacia, anise, benzoin, broom, comfrey, elder, eucalyptus, eyebright, hazel, lavender, lemon verbena, marjoram, mastic, mistletoe, mugwort, nutmeg, peppermint, sandalwood, spearmint, thyme, wormwood

Fire—*will; passion; divine within; energy; protection:* healing alder, angelica, basil, bay laurel, betony, carnation, celadine, cinnamon, coriander, cumin, garlic, holly, hyssop, juniper, marigold, peony, pepper, primrose, rosemary, rowan, rue, saffron, St. Johnswort, thistle, vervain

Water—*emotions; subconscious; dreams; purification; blood; fluids:* apple, ash, burdock, catnip, chamomile, cypress, elecampane, geranium, henbane, hyacinth, ivy, meadowsweet, myrrh, orris root, poppy, rose, star anise, willow, yarrow

Elemental Tides Correspondences

Earth—*12/21 (Winter Solstice) to 3/20 (Eve of Spring Equinox):* Planning; Cleansing, a time of preparation; North; Night; Midnight/ 12:00 A.M.; Old Age; Green; Physical Strength; the Body; Material Matters; Career; Wealth

Air—*3/21 (Spring Equinox) to 6/20 (Eve of Summer Solstice):* Beginnings, a time of initialization; East; Morning; Sunrise/6:00 A.M.; Childhood; Yellow; Intellect; Mind; Conscious; Breath; Psychic Power

Fire—*6/21 (Summer Solstice) to 9/22 (Eve of Autumn Equinox):* Harvest, Reaping, a time of fruition, completion; South; Midday; Noon/12:00 P.M.; Youth; Red; Will; Heart; Passion; Energy; Healing

Water—*9/23 (Autumn Equinox) to 12/20 (Eve of Winter Solstice):* Destruction, Replacement, rest, renewal, and passage; West; Afternoon; Sunset/6:00 P.M.; Maturity; Blue; Emotion; Fluids and Blood; Subconscious; Purification; Dreams

Appendix A

Color Correspondences

Amber—developing Witchcraft skills, empowerment

Black—ward negativity, remove hexes, protection, spirit contact, the universe, night, truth, remove discord or confusion

Blue (dark)—the Goddess (representational ritual candle), Water Elemental, truth, dreams, protection, change, meditation, impulse

Blue (light)—psychic awareness, intuition, opportunity, understanding, quests, safe journey, patience, tranquillity, ward depression, health

Brown—Earth Elemental, endurance, animal health, steadiness, houses and homes, physical objects, uncertainties

Gold—the God, solar energy, power, physical strength, success, skills sought, achievement, mental growth, healing energy, intuition, divination

Gray—non-Nature type Fairie magics such as communication with the Fairie Realms, travel to Otherworld, vision quests, veiling, neutralizing

Green—Lord and Lady of Wildwood, Earth Elemental, herb magics, Nature-type Fairie magics (such as blessing a garden), luck, fertility, healing, balance, employment, prosperity, courage, agriculture, changing direction or attitudes

Greenish-yellow—discord, sickness, anger, jealousy (use to negate these)

Indigo—meditation, spirit communication, Karma workings, learn the ancient wisdom, neutralize baneful magic, ward slander

Lavender—spiritual development, psychic growth, divination, sensitivity to Otherworld, blessings

Orange—the God (representational ritual candle) strength, healing, pulling things to you, adaptability, luck, vitality, encouragement, clearing the mind, dominance

Pink—honor, morality, friendships, emotional love

Purple—power, spiritual development, intuition, ambition, healing, progress, business, spiritual communication, protection, occult wisdom

Red—Fire Elemental, strength, power, energy, health, vigor, enthusiasm, courage, passion, sexuality

Silver—the Goddess, Lunar magics, meditation, psychic development, success, balance, wards negativity

Variegated—inner development through relaxation and introspection

Violet—self-improvement, intuition, success in searches

White—the Lady and the Lord together, Full Moon magics, purity, protection, truth, meditation, peace, sincerity, justice, wards doubts and fears

Yellow—Air Elemental, divination, clairvoyance, mental alertness, intellectual growth, prosperity, learning, changes, harmony, creativity

Planetary Correspondences

Sun—individuality, pride, display, success, honors, energy, power

Moon—personality, sensitivity, emotions, desires, start/end of cycles, projects, intuition, contentment

Mercury—communication, skill, agility, sensory impressions, thinking, learning

Venus—sociability, love, friendships, emotions, artistry, values, money, luxuries

Mars—dynamic energy, aggressiveness, willpower, sex drive, initiative

Saturn—ambition, structure, realism, self-preservation, business, self-control, restrictions/freedom, materiality

Jupiter—optimism, opportunity, health, expansion, finances, wealth, idealism, justice

Neptune—occultism, sub-conscious, psychic energy, spirit, Otherworld, idealism, creativity, illusion

Pluto—transformation, sex, death, rebirth, the soul, evolution, Underworld, extremes, spirituality, life cycle free from bondage

Uranus—sudden and unpredictable changes, tensions, news, originality, knowledge, innovation, divination

Planetary Hours for Day and Night

Here is how to create your own chart indicating the planetary influence for each hour of the day (or use one from a source such as Llewellyn's *Magical Almanac*). Put the days of the week across the top of your chart, and the hours of the day down the left side headed as Sunrise Hours 1 through 12 and Sunset Hours 1 through 12. The planetary sequence begins according to the ruling planet of the day and follows in the same order in a column under each day: Sunday begins with the Sun in the first hour after Sunrise, then continues with Venus, Mercury, Moon, Saturn, Jupiter, Mars, each allotted the next hour in sequence, then repeat the cycle. For Sunday, as an example, the first hour after sunrise is the Sun, the second hour is ruled by Venus, and so forth. The hours after sunset simply continue the sequence *uninterrupted* (the twelfth hour of sunrise is Saturn, the first hour of sunset is Jupiter). Go to the next column under Monday and begin with the Moon and follow the sequence. Tuesday starts with Mars, Wednesday with Mercury, Thursday with Jupiter, Friday with Venus, and Saturday with Saturn. This chart is something you will refer to regularly for the timing of your spells.

Correspondences for Daily Influences

Monday—*planet:* Moon; *colors:* silver, white, gray; *herbs:* moonwort; myrtle, violet, willow, wormwood; *influences:* dreams, emotions, clairvoyance, home, family, medicine, cooking, personality, merchandising, theft

Tuesday—*planet:* Mars; *colors:* red, orange; *herbs:* basil, dragon's blood, patchouli; *influences:* dynamic energy, matrimony, war, enemies, prison, hunting, surgery, courage, politics, contests

Wednesday—*planet:* Mercury; *colors:* gray, iridescent, opal, violet, yellow; *herbs:* jasmine, lavender; *influences:* communication, loss, teaching, reason, divination, skill, debt, fear, self-improvement

Thursday—*planet:* Jupiter; *colors:* blue, indigo, purple; *herbs:* cinnamon, cinquefoil, musk, nutmeg, sage; *influences:* health, honor, luck, riches, clothing, money, legal matters, desires

Friday—*planet:* Venus; *colors:* aqua, green, pink; *herbs:* lime, saffron, sandalwood, thyme; *influences:* love, friendship, social activities, strangers, pleasure, art, music, incense and perfumes

Saturday—*planet:* Saturn; *colors:* black, dark gray, indigo; *herbs:* black poppy seeds, mullein, myrrh; *influences:* self-discipline, life, building, doctrine, protection, freedom, elderly, destroying diseases and pests

Sunday—*planet:* Sun; *colors:* gold, orange, white, yellow; *herbs:* frankincense, lemon, St. Johnswort; *influences:* individuality, hope, fortune, money, work, power, healing, promotions, strength, spirituality

Numerical Correlations

1=the letters A, J, S; Sun; Fire; Developing the Self, the All, Beginning and Ending; Wholeness and Unity

2=the letters B, K, T; Moon; Water; Sensitivity and Personality, Truth, Blessing, Duality; Balance

3=the letters C, L, U; Jupiter; Fire; Health and Opportunity, Triads and Triple Aspects; Career

4=the letters D, M, V; Uranus; Air; Divination and Knowledge, Quarters, Firmness, Strength; Foundations; The Elementals

5=the letters E, N, W; Mercury; Air; Communication, 5-fold Aspect of the Pentagram (4 Elementals + Spirit); Fulfillment

6=the letters F, O, X; Venus; Earth; Sociability and Emotions, Unity of Triple Goddess and Triple God, Magnetism, Cats; Decisions

7=the letters G, P, Y; Neptune; Water; Subconscious, Intuition, Psychic Power, Mysticism, Dual Triads as a Unity; Change

8=the letters H, Q, Z; Saturn; Earth; Freedom, Dual Foundations, Material and Spiritual Worlds, Law, Self-discipline; Travel/News

9=the letters I, R; Mars; Fire; Aggression, Energy, New Path, Immortality, Indestructibility; Binding to Completion

Runic Tables

Rune Letter	Meaning and Use	Colors
Osa ᚠ (A)	the God; good fortune; favorable outcome	green/white
As ᚨ (AE)	ancestor; signs; gain ancient wisdom	indigo/purple
Beorc ᛒ (B)	Goddess; fertility; growth; new beginnings	white/green
Daeg ᛟ (D)	daybreak; between the worlds; breakthrough	pale violet
Eh ᛗ (E)	movement; safe journey; progress; changes	blue
Feoh ᚡ (F)	material wealth; fulfillment; ambition satisfied	green
Gefu ✕ (G)	union; partnership; love; gifts; self-confidence	pink/red
Eoh ᛄ (GH)	a channel; action; Otherworld communication	indigo/purple
Haegl ᚺ (H)	hail; limits/disruptions; awakening	white/blue
Is ᛁ (I)	ice; immobility; rest period; stop slander	white/silver
Gera ᛇ (J)	year; harvest; rewards; tangible results from work	white/green
Ken ᚲ (K/C)	transforming fire; opening energy; fresh start	white/gold
Lagu ᛚ (L)	fluidity; water; psychic power; intuition; vitality	blue/violet
Mannaz ᛗ (M)	Self; self-improvement; cooperation; meditation	indigo/violet
Nyd ᚾ (N)	constraint; self-control; overcome obstacles	white/blue
Ing ᛜ (NG)	the Horned God; fertility; family; completion	indigo

Runic Tables, continued

Rune Letter	Meaning and Use	Colors
Ethel ⊗ (OE)	possession; home; social status; acquisitions	white/gold
Perth ⊼ (P)	destiny; hidden forces; unexpected luck; initiation	blue/green
Rad ᚱ (R)	travel; quest; find what is sought; attunement	blue/violet
Sigel ᛰ (S)	sun wheel; wholeness; healing; vital energy; power	orange/gold
Tyr ↑ (T)	victory; success; courage; favorable outcome	white/gold
Thorn þ (TH)	protection; gateway; foes neutralized; defense	black
Uruz ᚢ (U)	strength; physical health; courage; promotion	green/brown
Wyn ᚹ (W)	joy; comfort; happiness; harmony; love	pink/yellow
Eolh ᛉ (Z)	elk; protection; friendship; going unnoticed	white
Wyrd [ ] (/)	unknowable fate; destiny; cosmic influence	black/white

Symbolism for Divination

Acorn—youth, strength, man, small start for large accomplishment

Airplane—travel, new projects

Anchor—voyage, rest, problem solved

Arrow—news, disagreements, direct action

Basket—gift, security, comfort

Baby—new interests, security, new beginnings

Bees (hive, comb)—fertility, industry, community, self-sacrifice

Bell—celebrations, news (good or bad depending on other indicators)

Bird—psychic power, flight, luck, friendship end, communication

Boat—discoveries, travel, companionship

Book—wisdom, learning

Bottle—celebration, success

Broom—Goddess, purification, healing, end of a problem, changes

Bridge—crossing to new endeavors, transition, partnership, travel

Butterfly—the soul, spiritual contact, frivolity, insincerity

Castle—financial gain, security, inheritance, life of bounty

Cage—isolation, restriction, imprisonment, containment

Camel—long journey, need to conserve energy or goods, relocation

Cat—wisdom, spiritual access, female friend, domestic strife

Car—local travel, movement in business affairs, overcome obstacles

Cauldron—Goddess, transformation, endings/new beginnings, vitality

Candle—illumination, innovation, inspiration

Clock—time indicated for a spell's completion, change

Chair—relaxation, pause, comfort, entertainment

Clouds—mental activity, thoughtfulness, problems, hidden obstacles

Coffin—end of a matter, lengthy but not serious illness

Clover—good fortune, success, rural location

Cow—money, property, comfort, tranquillity

Cradle—newcomers, beginning of a new idea or project

Crescent—Goddess, wish granted, newness, freshness

Cornucopia—Goddess, abundance, fertility, prosperity, protection

Cross—(Solar) God, nature works with power; (Roman) suffering, conflict

Cup—love, harmony, close friendship, gift

Dagger—complications, dangers, power, skill

Death/dying—birth, marriage, long life, prosperity

Distaff—creativity, changes, sexuality

Dog—fidelity, friendship, companionship, faithfulness

Duck—plenty, wealth, success

Elephant—advice needed, obstacles overcome, good luck

Egg—increase, fertility, luck, creativity, new start, hoarding

Eye—introspection, awareness, evaluation, spirit

Fan—indiscretion, disloyalty, things hidden, inflammations

Fish—riches, luck, sexuality, productivity

Flag—warning, defensiveness, identification with group/ideals

Flame, fire—purification, change, domination of the will

Flower—marriage, unhappy love affair, passing joy

Glove—protection, luck, aloofness, nobility, challenge

Gate—opportunity, advancement, change, new directions

Gun (any type)—power to gain goals, discord, slander, infidelity

Hammer—hard work rewarded, building, creativity, fortitude

Hat—honors, rivalry, independence, self-assertion

Hound—advice, help given, companionship, trust

Heart—love, pleasure, confidence, strength of will

Harp—contentment, spirituality

Horns—God, fertility, spirituality, forces of nature

Horse—travel, strength, work, grace, power, success, prosperity

Horseshoe—protection, luck, start of a new enterprise

Hourglass—caution, passage of time

House—security, authority, success, comfort

Key—understanding, mysteries, opportunity, gain, security

Kite—warning for caution, new ideas, plans made public

Knot—restrictions, marriage, bindings

Knife—duplicity, misunderstanding, direct action

Ladder—initiation, rise or fall in status, connections

Lion—power, strength, influence, ferocity, pride, domination

Lock—protection, concealment, security, obstacles, sealed

Man—visitor, helpful stranger

Mirror—reversal, knowledge, Karma

Moon—the Goddess, intuitive wisdom, guidance

Mountain—hindrance, challenge, obstacle, journey, steadfastness

Mouse—poverty, theft, frugality, inconspicuousness

Mushroom—shelter, food, business complications, Fairy contact

---

Nail—labor, construction, pain, unity

Owl—wisdom, spiritual communication

Palm tree—respite, relief, security, protection, blessings

Parrot—gossip, ostentatiousness

Peacock—luxury, vanity, arrogance—all with little foundation

Pineapple—hospitality, good things hidden by harsh exterior

Pipe—truth obscured, concentration, comfort, ease

Purse—monetary gain, possessions kept close

Ring—eternity, containment, wheel of life/year, wedding

Rose—love, lost or past love, fullness of life, healing, caring

Salt—purity, stability, cleansing, grounding

Scales—balance, justice, careful evaluation

Scissors—duplicity, arguments, separation, division, strife

Shell—Goddess, emotional stability, luck, artistic ability

Ship—travel, news, material gains, romance

Skull—consolation, comfort, personal hurts, endings and a new life

Snake—God and Goddess, wisdom, immortality, knowledge, prophecy

Spider—good luck, industry, entrapments, secrecy, cunning

Spoon—luck, sustenance, the basic needs of life secured

Sun—the God, success, energy, power

Star—good luck, divine protection, opportunity, success, destiny

Swan—good luck, love, evolving beauty, noble spirit

Sword—power, strife, conflict, overcoming adversity

Tree—blessings of Nature, good fortune, stability, power, security

Turtle—fertility, security, defense against obstacles, slow gains

Umbrella—temporary shelter, limited protection

Unicorn—purity, nature, Fairy blessings, Otherworld intervention

Well—blessing from the Goddess, inspiration, spirituality, health

Wheel—completion, eternity, season/life cycles, rebirth, gains

Windmill—business dealings, factors working together for one goal

Magical Stones and Crystals

(Elixir Benefits)

Agate—health, good fortune, eloquence, vitality/energy, self-confidence, bursts of mental/physical energy, balance emotions, calm body/mind/emotions

Banded—relieve stress

Blue-Lace—calm, third eye, self-expression, neutralize anger; (encourage trust and friendliness)

White with Blue/Black Spots—travel

Eye Formation—bodily protection, travel

Mossy—healing, cleansing, strength, abundance, self-confidence, harmony, release anger/frustration, earth-energies connection

Milky with Red—visualization skills, gain goals

Alexandrite—balance the nervous system, color therapy

Amazonite—good fortune, female power, soothe nervous system, improve thought process, regulate metabolism; (social ability)

Amber—strengthen/break spell—a Witch stone, increase, success, health, healing, love, absorb negative energy, manifestation, good luck; (relief from despair)

Amethyst—spirituality, protection from negativity through transformation, intuition, dreams, relieve tension, meditation, cleansing/energizing, protect against psychic manipulation; (help in compromise)

Apache Tear—protection from directed negative energies, grounding energies, spiritual meditation

Apatite—strengthen muscles, coordination

Aqua-Aura—meditation, release of emotional tension

Aquamarine—psychological influence, inspire thought process, good luck in tests, positive interviews; (calms; relieves tension)

Auricalcite—calm, clear away tension, neutralize anger

Aventurine—creativity, luck in physical activities, courage, calm, sleep, leadership, decision-making; (soothe eyes; gain an open mind; curb pride/aloofness)

Azurite (blended blues and greens)—psychic development; meditation; facing fears, healing, visions (help in controlling own reality)

Beryl—intellect, will-power, aid heart/digestive system; (build self-esteem)

Bloodstone (Heliotrope)—remove obstacles, vitality, enhance talents, balance, health/healing, ward injury, purify the blood, courage, strength, integrity; (curb obsessive affection)

Boji Stone (paired: one smooth/other bumpy with projections)— strengthen chakras, healing, regenerative, balance energy fields

Calcite—*Gold*—healing, cheerfulness; (reach for new goals/emotional contacts)

Green—soothe fears, calm, aid intuition, transitions

Orange—physical energy, expand awareness, intuition

Carnelian—career success, fast action, shield thoughts, good health, protection, grounding, motivation, personal power

Chalcedony—optimism, spiritual/artistic creativity

Chalcopyrite (Peacock Stone)—alleviate worry, focus for prosperity, happiness, protect from negativity

Chrysocolla—balance, cleanse negativity, contentment, healing, prosperity, good luck, clears mind; (open a path away from daily routine)

Chrysoprase—peace, meditation, clairvoyance, gain incentive; (temper egotism)

Citrine—success, clear thinking, protection, direction, induce dreams, improve self-image/confidence, prosperity, manifest personal power, initiative, creativity, endurance

Coral—calm, relaxation, protect from illness, ward unwanted thought energies

Diamond—protection, avert unseen danger, emotional healer, power, purity, strength

Dioptase—relaxation, relieve stress, overcome emotional loss

Dolomite—avert fear of failure; (focus on success/gain resourcefulness)

Emerald—artistic talent, memory, truth, visions, business success, peace, love, psychic insight, tranquillity

Fluorite—meditation, Fairy Realms, dreams, past lives, aids intellect, heals energy drains in the aura, ground/balance/focus energy, absorb/alter negative energy; discernment, aid concentration

Garnet—swift movement, balance energies, revitalization, self-esteem/confidence, dreamwork, energy/courage, love/bonding, devotion

Geodes—freedom of spirit, linking with the cosmic dance

Hematite—communication skills, astral projection, balance/focus energy, clear/calm reasoning, draw good relationships; (diminish defenselessness)

Herkimer Diamond—relieve stress, power booster for crystals/bojis, dream interpretation, psychic attunement; (gain goals, freer expression of love)

Iron Pyrite—attract success, health/wealth/happiness, intellect, creativity, psychic development, channeling, memory

Jacinth—spiritual insight

Jade—peace, cleansing, harmony, friendship, good luck, protection, safe travel, wisdom, long life, dream focus/content; (realistic/practical ideals)

Jasper—strengthen energy flow, relieve stress, gather energy for directing, nurturing, protection, grounding, safe astral travel

Red—returns negativity to sender; defensive magics

Brown—grounding and stability; soothes nerves

Green—healing and fertility

Jet—bind energy to a goal—a Witch stone, calm fears, protection

Kunzite—meditation, balance negative emotions, purification, Divine connection

Kyanite—meditation, past lives recall, channeling, vivid dreams, visualization, altered states, serenity, manifestation of thought into reality

Lapis Lazuli—authority, power booster, aura cleanser, psychic development, mental balance, self-awareness, inner truths/wisdom, access universal knowledge

Larimar—transmute negative energies like anger/greed/frustration, bring excessive energies into balance

Lazurite—visions

Magnetite (Howlite)—meditation, tranquillity, calm fear/anger, honesty

Malachite—business success, protection, vision quest, meditation, prosperity, hope, health, happiness, avert confusion/apathy, manifest desires; (ease focus for controlling reality)

Moldavite (meteorite stone)—transformation, star communication, heal longing, find life purpose, dimensional travel; (decision making, confidence, re-focusing)

Moonstone—psychic ability, divination, love, comfort, peace, long life, friends, inspiration, draw attachment/sensitivity, wish granting, new start; (ease in surroundings, curb spending)

Morion Crystal—nearly black crystal used for grounding energies

Obsidian—*Black*—protection, scrying, Dark Aspect meditation, Otherworld contact, Shadowland contact, banish grief, benevolence, healing

Green—protection of income; open financial opportunities

Snowflake—grounding, responsibility, purification, change, growth, deflect negative energy

Onyx—equilibrium, end worry, justice, concentration, devotion, guidance through dreams/meditation, balance of duality

Black—deal with emotions/frustration

Opal—psychic power, astral travel, meditation, calm, direct thoughts inward, reflect what is sent, shape-shifting, invisibility; (relaxation, calmative)

Pearl—astral projection, dreams; (ease fears, calm the nerves)

Peridot—soulmates, clairvoyance, solar power, attract occult power, inner vision, open awareness, ward negativity, body tonic

Petrified Wood—past lives recall, physical energy, preservation of strength, firmness of stance, serenity, balance, grounding, vitality

Pumice—power, manifestation

Quartz Crystal—psychic power, vision quest, protection, energy, divination, projection, attain goals, cleanse aura, meditation, intuition, store/focus/direct/transmit energy; (protection)

Blue—release emotional tension, soothe

Rock Crystal—scrying; energizing; water magics

Rose—peace, love, comfort, companionship; (self-discipline, responsibility)

Rutilated—increase strength of will; (control self-indulgence)

Smoky—generate energy, protection, purify energies, Fairy connection, disperse negative/draw positive energy; (personal interactions)

Snow—meditation, serenity, peace, contemplation

Rhodochrosite—generate energy, physical/emotional balance, heal trauma, union of male/female aspects; (regain emotional energy after frustrations)

Rhodinite—self-esteem, physical energy, self-actualization, service; (ease physical fatigue, negate fear of criticism)

Ruby—protect health/wealth, increase energy/creativity, self-confidence, intuition, contentment, courage, spiritual wisdom, generate heat

Sapphire—wisdom, material gains, attract good influences, peace of mind, hope

Sardonyx—draw troubles then toss stone into the sea, self-protection

Selenite—calming for meditation/visualization, clarify thoughts, healing; (overcome guilt, let go of negativity, curb over-active fantasizing)

Sodalite—meditation, enhance memory, relieve stress, aid sleep, enhance logical thought, stimulate intellect; (control rage, curb need for negative attention)

Staurolite (Fairy Cross)—good luck, protection, security, manifesting higher self on earth plane, astral connection, confidence

Sugilite—logic, business expertise, astral travel, manifestation, self-healing

Sunstone—energy, healing, success

Tiger Eye—good luck, objectivity, truth, self-confidence, protection from ill will of others, harmony, grounding, stability, instinctive/psychic ability, wisdom, healing; (builds self-confidence)

Topaz—*Blue*—psychic insight, spiritual growth, leadership, concentration, clarity of thought

Yellow—stress, deep sleep, psychic ability, calm body/mind, fulfillment of dreams/wishes by focusing into the facets, intentional creation, healing, prosperity, other realms, revitalize bodily energies; (commitment to action, building willpower and decisiveness)

Tourmaline—beauty, freshness, joy, friendship, grounding, protection, calm, attract goodwill, self-confidence, discernment, inspiration; (elixir by type)

Black—redirect restlessness into productivity

Blue—clear speech, unblock mind/emotion, rubbing generates an electrical charge to direct energy

Green/Black—prosperity/deflect negative energies

Green—setting reasonable goals

Pink—encourage creativity, free the personality

Watermelon—encourage practical approach to manifesting ideas

Watermelon/Pink—self understanding

Turquoise—verbal communication, put thoughts into words, protect the spirit, health, love, joy, social life, meditation, intuition, unify spiritual/physical; (open awareness, find creative solutions to problems, curb fear of the dark)

Unikite—grounding, balance, stability

Viviante (Rare)—rebirth, clear-sightedness, enlightenment

Zircon—spiritual sight, spiritual understanding

Appendix B

CASTING AND OPENING THE CIRCLE

Casting the Circle

1. Lay out the circle and altar items. A warm bath, scented perhaps with fragrant bath salts or an herbal bouquet, will help set the mood, soothing away the cares of the day and allowing the intuitional senses to come forward. Robe in something comfortable and loose, perhaps something you set aside only for use in ritual so that your mind instinctively recognizes a change in the daily routine and relaxes. Ground and center, push the static energies out through your feet to be able to now find the calm within, stabilizing your energy flow and envisioning the energy of the Earth coming up through your feet to intertwine with your own energy for a smooth flow of power. Remember that the circle is intended to provide a sacred space and retain raised energy until such time as you release it to achieve a goal. The circle does not absorb or hold onto negative energies, but acts as a buffer that repels negativity away. When you open the circle, you draw the circle's energy back into yourself then drain the residue into the ground, retaining only your own energy, and any necessary energy to keep yourself in balance.

2. Sweep the circle area with a besom (witch's broom), herbal sprig, or leafy twig:

   I sweep away from this space all negative and discordant energies that I may focus and raise the energy I need for my work. Let this space be made clear for my circle.

3. Light incense and candles (number is up to you, but you may want to use three on the altar for the Lady on the left, the Lord on the right, and Both at the center; one additional candle may be lit to carry to the Quarters and used to light the votive or working candle, or the center candle may be used for these).

4. Ring the bell or clap hands three times:

   The circle is about to be cast and I freely stand within to greet my Lady and my Lord.

5. Take the center or altar candle and use it to light a candle for each of the Elementals, or simply pause at each compass point and raise this candle as you walk around the circle going North, East, South, and West. If lighting candles at the Quarters, use green for Earth at the North, then yellow for Air at the East, red for Fire at the South, and blue for Water at the West:

   (N) *I call upon Light and Earth at the North to illuminate and strengthen the circle.*

   (E) *I call upon Light and Air at the East to illuminate and enliven the circle.*

   (S) *I call upon Light and Fire at the South to illuminate and warm the circle.*

   (W) *I call upon Light and Water at the West to illuminate and cleanse the circle.*

6. With your ritual knife held up, pace the circle moving around from the North to the East to the South to the West, and to the North:

   I draw this circle in the presence of the Goddess and the God where they may come and bless their child, _____. (State either your given name, or a Craft Name. If alone and you have one, state your secret Working Name with whom they have named, _____.)

Now lower the athame at the North, and as you walk around the circle, envision a blue light shooting out from the point and forming the circle boundary:

This is the boundary of the circle. Only love shall enter and leave.

7. Return to the altar and ring the bell or clap three times

8. Place point of your athame in the salt:

   Salt is life and purifying. I bless this salt to be used in this sacred circle in the names of the Goddess and the God, _____ (you can add here the names you use: Shakti and Shiva; Hecate and Herne; Bendidia and Pan; Freya and Frey; Isis and Osiris are examples).

9. Pick up the salt bowl and use tip of the athame to drop three portions of salt into the water bowl; set the salt bowl back in its place.

10. Stir three times with the athame:

    Let the blessed salt purify this water that it may be sanctified for use in this sacred circle. In the names of the Goddess and the God (N and N). I consecrate and cleanse this water.

11. Take the salted water bowl in hand and sprinkle water from it as you move deosil (clockwise) around the circle (N-E-S-W-N):

    I consecrate this circle in the names of the Goddess and the God, (N and N). The circle is conjured a Circle of Power that is purified and sealed. So Mote It Be!

12. Return the water bowl to the altar and take the incense around the circle (N-E-S-W-N):

    Let this aroma and smoke purify the atmosphere within the circle that it may be pleasing and welcoming.

13. With a dab of anointing oil on your finger, make a Solar Cross (equal-armed, like a plus sign) ringed by a circle on your forehead:

*I, (N) am consecrated in the names of the Goddess and the
God (N and N), in this their circle.*

14. Invoking the Elementals begins at the North, and moves
    deosil around the circle. You may want to use the wand or
    your power hand to do the invoking, and additionally you
    may want to draw in the air an appropriate invoking (and
    when opening the circle, a departing) pentagram. The
    pentagrams are easy to remember when you envision the
    star, tracing the image in the air with the starting point being
    that of the direction you are in and continuing with one line
    to finish the rest of the image. So at the North for Elemental
    Earth, begin at the top of the star and move to the South,
    down the left slope of the point, continuing to draw the rest
    of the star. At the East for Elemental Air, begin at the right
    arm of the star, moving across the star to the West, continuing
    to form the rest of the star. At the South for Elemental Fire,
    begin at the right foot of the star, moving to the North along
    the right slope and continuing to draw the rest of the star. At
    the West for Elemental Water, start on the left arm of the star,
    moving across the star to the East, then continuing to form
    the rest of the star. When opening the circle, reverse the
    directions. For Earth, begin at the left foot of the star and
    move to the North, and continue the star. For Air, begin at
    the western left arm and move to the East, then finish the star.
    For Fire, begin at the northern point and move to the right
    foot of the star, then finish the design. For Water, begin at
    eastern right arm and move to the West, then finish drawing
    the star. Without the drawing of pentacles in the air, you sim-
    ply hold up the wand with both arms upraised, at the North
    of the circle during the same invocation (envision a powerful
    bull arriving):

    *I call upon you, Elemental Earth, to attend this rite and
    guard this circle, for as I have body and strength, we are kith
    and kin!*

15. Lower the wand and move to the East; raise the wand (see an owl, Fairies, or an eagle in flight):

    I call upon you, Elemental Air, to attend this rite and guard this circle, for as I breathe and think, we are kith and kin!

16. Lower the wand and move to the South, raise the wand (see a lion, salamander, or dragon):

    I call upon you, Elemental Fire, to attend this rite and guard this circle, for as I consume life to live, we are kith and kin!

17. Lower the wand and move to the West, hold wand aloft (see an undine, a sea serpent, or a dolphin):

    I call upon you, Elemental Water, to attend this rite and guard this circle, for as I feel and my heart beats, we are kith and kin!

18. Return to the altar and use your wand to draw the lemniscate (infinity symbol that looks like a figure 8 on its side) in the air above the altar—the sign of working between the worlds.

19. Set your wand on the altar and raise up the athame in both hands:

    Hail to the Elementals at the Four Quarters! I welcome thee Lady and Lord to this rite! I stand between the worlds with Love and Power all around!

20. Ring bell or clap three times. The circle is cast and you may now perform your ritual. During some rituals, such as with an Esbat, in which you may be conducting spell work, you will be making a libation (offering) of wine (or other beverage) and cake (or other grain product) to the Divine, and so you will have these items on the altar (see Appendix C for a suggested layout). Otherwise, follow your ritual with a snack and beverage that may be part of a Cakes and Wine ritual (see example in Appendix D).

Opening the Circle

1. Ring the bell or clap three times.

2. Hold your athame level over the altar:

   Lord and Lady, I am blessed by your sharing this time with me; watching and guarding me; guiding me here and in all things. Your love and blessings continue with me even after the ending of this rite, and so do my love and blessings return unto you both as a never-ending circle of communion, for you are always with me. In love have I come into this ritual, and in love do I depart.

3. Raise the athame in a salute:

   Love is the Law and Love is the Bond. Merry did we meet, merry do we part, and merry will we meet again. Merry meet, merry part, and merry meet again! The circle is now cleared. So Mote It Be!

4. Kiss the flat of the blade and set the athame on the altar.

5. Take the snuffer and go to the North Quarter, and with raised arms:

   Depart in peace, Elemental Earth. My blessings take with you!

   Lower your arms, crossing your chest, then uncross as you now snuff the candle and envision the Elemental Power departing. If using an invoking pentagram, then say your farewell, draw the departing pentagram, and snuff the candle.

6. Go to the East, raise your arms:

   Depart in peace, Elemental Air. My blessings take with you!

   Lower arms and snuff the candle; envision the Elemental Power departing.

7. Go to the South, raise your arms:

   Depart in peace, Elemental Fire. My blessings take with you!

Lower arms and snuff the candle; envision the Elemental Power departing.

8. Go to the West, raise your arms:

   Depart in peace, Elemental Water. My blessings take with you!

   Lower arms and snuff the candle; envision the Elemental Power departing.

9. Return to the altar; set down snuffer and raise your arms in benediction:

   Beings and powers of the visible and invisible, you aid in my work, whisper in my mind, and bless me from Otherworld. There will always be harmony between us. Depart in peace, and my blessings take with you. The circle is cleared.

10. Take the athame and go to the North Quarter. Point the athame down and move widdershins (counter-clockwise) around the circle starting at the North and ending at the North, envisioning the blue light being drawn back into the athame:

    The circle is open yet the circle remains as its magical power is drawn back into me.

    When you return to the North, having walked the circle, touch the athame lightly to your forehead, and envision the blue light swirling around back into you. Do not be concerned about the excess energy at this point as you will be grounding it very soon.

11. You should now be at the altar:

    The ritual is ended. Blessings have been given and blessings have been received. May the peace of the Goddess and the God remain in my heart. So Mote It Be!

12. Set down the athame. Put away all the magical tools and clear the altar. Dispose of spell materials and any libation materials. Touch the palms of your hands to the ground (floor) to drain

off the excess energy. If you did not have a Cakes and Wine ritual, now is the time to have a snack and beverage to replenish your energy and bring you thoroughly back into the here and now.

Appendix C

Consecration
of a Tool

Altar

The altar may be decorated as you feel appropriate, with something to represent the Goddess and the God, such as statues, candles, a shell and a stone, crystals, and so forth. The arrangement of the altar falls into three sections, represented by the Goddess at the left, the God at the right, and the Divine as united in the center, and this is generally as shown here:

Goddess	Both	God
	Candelabra	
Statue/Object	Statue/Object	Statue/Object
Chalice		Censer
Water Bowl	Pentacle	Salt Bowl
Wand	Cauldron	Athame
Bell	Offering Dish	Bolline
Supplies	Book of Shadows	Food & Supplies
(oils, herbs)	(spell work materials)	(matches, incense)

Consecration Ritual

Tools of the Craft are usually consecrated during a Full Moon Esbat ritual, and you should have a red candle and a small bowl of fresh (not salted) water on the altar reserved for this. Your altar should already have a pentacle on it, and you should already have incense lit, but you may want to light a fresh stick, cone, or drop a fresh batch on a charcoal disk when you begin the consecration. After casting the circle, and invoking the Goddess, you proceed into your Esbat ritual. When that is completed, you may then work your spells, do meditations and divinations, and attend to other magical matters. The tool being consecrated should simply rest on the altar during your Esbat ritual, soaking up some of the energy from your ceremony. Now you inscribe it with magical signs and symbols of your choosing, and perhaps with your Craft Name written in runic letters. Light the red candle and fresh incense. Hold up the tool over the altar:

> *In the Names of the Goddess and the God, (_____), I*
> *consecrate this* (name of item) *to be used in my practice*
> *of the Craft. I charge this by Elemental Earth* (touch the
> object to the pentacle); *by Elemental Air* (pass it through
> the incense smoke); *by Elemental Fire* (pass it quickly
> through the flame of the red candle); *and by Elemental*
> *Water* (sprinkle the tool with the fresh water). *This tool is*
> *now by Powers Elemental and Divine bond to aid me in my*
> *work. So Mote It Be!*

Now you are ready to proceed to the Cakes and Wine Ceremony (Appendix D), and to the opening of the circle (Appendix A). Use your new tool, then wrap and store it with your other magical items, being sure not to let other people handle it. If it is handled, then do another consecration, first cleansing it through the blessed water (salted), followed by passing the tool through the symbols of the Elementals.

Appendix D

CAKES AND WINE

After the Ritual/Before
Opening the Circle

When doing a ritual, either for spell work or as a Sabbat or Esbat celebration, the circle is cast (see Appendix A) and the ritual is conducted, followed by Cakes and Wine for part of the grounding process. This is both a ritual of communion with the Divine and an opportunity to begin your return to the mundane world. After casting the circle, you may have written your spell work or ritual to include a libation to the Goddess and the God, especially if doing spell work during an Esbat. This means that the beverage and food has been on the altar, in a chalice and on a small plate, and a libation bowl has been used to receive a little of the beverage and a pinch of the cake as offerings. Now the remainder of the meal is ready for you to use after your spell work. This meal is also called the Simple Feast, and when this is finished, you open the circle.

1. Ring bell or clap hands three times.

2. With feet spread and arms upraised before the altar:

   *I acknowledge my needs and offer my appreciation
   to that which sustains me! May I ever remember the
   blessings of my Lady and my Lord.*

3. Bring your feet back together, then take up goblet of beverage (wine, juice, or spring water) in your left hand and hold your athame in the right hand. Slowly lower the point of the athame into the wine:

   *As male joins female for the happiness of both, let
   the fruits of Their union promote life. Let the Earth*

197

be fruitful and let Her wealth be spread throughout
all lands.

4. Lay down the athame, pour a little water in the offering dish
   and take a drink from the goblet. Then replace the goblet on
   the altar, pick up the athame, and touch the point of the knife
   to the cake (roll, muffin, cupcake, or other such food):

   This food is the blessing of the Lady and the Lord given freely
   to me. As freely as I have received, may I also give food for
   the body, mind, and spirit to those who seek such of me.

5. Pinch off a piece of cake and add to the offering dish; eat the
   cake and finish the beverage:

   As I enjoy these gifts of the Goddess and the God, _____,
   may I remember that without Them I would have nothing.
   So Mote It Be!

6. Open the circle (see Appendix B).

Mail Order Supplies

AVALON
1211 Hillcrest Street
Orlando, FL 32803
(407) 895-7439
www.avalonbeyond.com
catalog: $3.00

DRYAD DESIGN
37 Commercial Drive, Suite 2
Waterbury, VT 05676
www.dryaddesign.com

EYE OF THE CAT
3314 E. Broadway
Long Beach, CA 90803
(310) 438-3569

EYE OF THE DAY
P. O. Box 21261
Boulder, CO 80308
1-800-717-3307

LINDA RAY RESEARCH
Importer Essential Oils/Lotions
(954) 583-2944
http://home.att.net/~LINDARAY/LINDARAY
   @worldnet.att.net

MAGIC BOOK STORE
2306 Highland Avenue
National City, CA 91950
(619) 477-5260

ROOTS AND WINGS
16607 Barberry, C2
Southgate, MI 48195
(313) 285-3679

WHITE LIGHT PENTACLES/
 SACRED SPIRIT PRODUCTS
P. O. Box 8163
Salem, MA 01971-8163

SACRED SOURCE
P. O. Box 163
Crozet, VA 22932
www.sacredsource.com

Glossary

Amulet—a natural object, such as a rabbit's foot or herbal pouch, carried or worn for protection and luck, a variety of charm.

Animistic—seeing all things as having a spirit, thus the Divine spirit resides in all things. Key phrase: everything is alive.

Astral Plane—an energy level of existence that lies outside the physical and mental planes of reality.

Athame—ritual black-handled (generally) knife that is not used as a cutting tool but to direct energy.

Aura—the energy field surrounding all things. It may be seen visually or sensed psychically, to be understood or manipulated in magic.

Besom—broom used to sweep the circle clear of negative and chaotic energies prior to casting.

Bindrune—a runic monogram of two to three rune symbols used as a sigil on a magical object, with the last rune binding the whole.

Blue Moon—second Full Moon in a solar month.

Bolline—white- or brown-handled (generally) knife used to cut and inscribe magical items.

BOS—Book of Shadows: the book or books in which correlations are written down and referenced in the creation of spells and other magics, containing a code of ethics, personal philosophy, spiritual insights, meditations, lunar and seasonal rituals, descriptions of tools, alphabets, recipes, rites of passage rituals, special days of observance, deity associations, and other details deemed necessary by the individual for the practice of the Craft.

Broom Closet—figurative way of describing whether a Witch prefers to keep Craft practice a secret or is more public about Craft activities, and is therefore, presumably with besom in hand, either in or out of the broom closet.

Ceremonial Magic—magic system based on the Hebrew Kabbalah of twelfth-century Europe.

Charged—energized, particularly imbued with Divine blessing as with holy (or blessed) water used in Witchcraft.

Charms—objects made and infused with magical energy to be carried or placed somewhere to achieve a goal such as protection, draw money, draw love.

Circle—a ritual area created to contain raised energy that may be directed in spell work. The energy is raised through the Earth and blended within the Witch, then directed to form the boundaries of the circle. When the circle is opened, the energy is returned into the Witch so that the borrowed energy can be directed into the Earth through touching for dissipation. This energy field does not act like static cling, holding negative energies in place, but is always pure and clean, simply repelling negative or chaotic energies from entering the sacred space.

Comparative Magic—the magical method of seeing one object acting in the stead of another, with the key phrase being, "This REPRESENTS that."

Contagion—a generally accepted sub-category of sympathetic magic in Wicca that requires the use of something that has been in touch with the object of the spell work.

Containment Magic—the magical purpose of holding a desired energy in one place, hence protection magics such as shielding, deflecting, and reflecting an energy influence.

Correspondences—correlations of magical energy to items of Nature, colors, hours of the day, days of the week, symbols, alphabetic interpretations, lunar and solar phases, and other such meanings to be used in creating or interpreting magical work.

Cosmic Lemniscate—the symbol of Infinity, like a number 8 on its side.

Craft Name—a name selected by the Witch for working in the Craft, and may be used among other like-minded people. This name may also be used as a coven name, although many covens prefer to re-name someone entering their circle.

Directive Magic—the magical method of moving the energy of one object to influence another, with the key phrase being, "This AFFECTS that."

Drawing Magic—the magical purpose of bringing something, hence enticing and invoking an energy influence.

Elementals—energy archetypes of the God and the Goddess expressed as individual entities and powers embodying the four elements of Earth, Air, Fire, and Water; emanations of Divine Power, respected and worked with in the focusing of energy, but not worshipped as the dictionary definition of elementalism.

Etheric Plane—an energy level of existence not on the physical plane, nor on the astral, but in between where it acts as a connecting passage.

Fairy Moon—see Sidhe Moon.

Familiar—the animal or spirit helper of a Witch.

Generator—a large crystal that is used in the charging of other crystals. Place the stone or crystal being charged on a pentacle, with the generator crystal on top of it, then conduct your consecration. This is a crystal that you often work through, forming a close energy relationship.

Green Witchcraft—foundation level of the Old Religion, grounded in Nature, approaching the Craft through the Elementals, the Other People, and the Goddess and the God, using herbs, natural objects, and Earth energy in spell crafting. The Divine is seen as the Lady and the Lord of the Wildwood, primarily as Earth Mother and Horned God, but also in their many other natural (rather than political) aspects, and thus the Craft is both animistic and pantheistic. The energies raised join internally with that of the Witch to be focused, directed, released, and sent to accomplish a goal.

Grimoires—books of magical formulas created by ceremonial magicians between the twelfth and sixteenth centuries in Europe, containing elaborate rituals based on Jewish and Christian dichotomy concepts of Heaven and Hell/good and evil/light and dark so that the numerous angels and demons are placed in hierarchical order to be summoned and banished according to the magician's will. There are names of power, lists of correspondences, seals and sigils, and other such information, for the working of magic by externally commanding these energies. Term now used also for the BOS.

Homeopathic—a generally accepted sub-category of sympathetic magic in Wicca that uses correlations in creating magic.

Kenned—an all-encompassing kind of knowing that is mentally understood, emotionally felt, and psychically sensed so that there is no doubt.

Magic—creating changes by the raising, focusing, directing, releasing, and sending of energy.

Mystic Moon—the Dark Moon seen as the Hidden Face of the Goddess. May be called the New Moon, unless referring to the thin Waning crescent.

Names of Power—names chanted for power-raising, derived from grimoires, from ancient deities' names, or invented in a frenzy of energy raising (rather like the Pentecostal practice of speaking in tongues).

Ogham—old Celtic alphabet symbols named for trees and shrubs, often used for their magical meanings as inscriptions and in divination.

Pantheistic—all energies and matter are aspects of the Divine, thus the Divine is manifested in everything. Key phrase: everything is Divine.

Repelling Magic—the magical purpose of casting something away, hence banishing or exorcising an energy influence, with purgings and releasings being lesser exorcisms.

Rituals—magical or devotional ceremonies in which energy is raised for Divine communion and/or the conducting of magic through spell work.

Runes—old Teutonic and Norse alphabet symbols often used as inscriptions for their magical meanings and in divination.

Saint's Days—holy days on the Catholic calendar, most of which are based upon prior existing Pagan holy days that the populace continued to celebrate into the European Middle Ages. These days were then Christianized by changing the focus to that of a saint, some of whom never existed, others of whom were local

Pagan deities addressed as living people who converted to Christianity, and others of whom were actual people named as saints by a formal Catholic procedure based on reports of miracles related to the individual.

Seals—magical diagrams using symbols, or using the numerical equivalents for names and planets in a square, perhaps with a sigil superimposed over it.

Sidhe Moon—second Dark Moon in a solar month and an opportune time for Otherworld and Fairy magics.

Sigils—a design drawn from linking with a continuous line the letters of a key word used as a focus in a magical working as the alphabetical letters appear on a wheel, square, rectangle, or triangle.

Speaking in Tongues—ecstatic speech during energy raising, in which the words are sounds that may be recognized as another language unknown to the speaker, or that express spiritual union directly without any language translation. This may occur during a drawing down of the Moon ritual in which the participant is filled with the spirit of the Goddess, or a drawing down of the Sun, in which the participant is filled with the spirit of the God.

Spells—energy gathered and directed in ritual to achieve a goal, thus spells are the vehicles of magical workings utilizing the movement of energy through the power of spoken word or formula, be it in a ritual, brew, charm, amulet, talisman, or crafted item created for magical purpose, generating intent into manifestation.

Sympathetic Magic—the magical method of seeing one object as another, with the key phrase being, "This IS that."

Talisman—an object such as a ring or pendant, usually engraved with magical symbols to bring good fortune, offer protection, ward misfortune, or some other such purpose. It is a variety of charm.

Transference Magic—the magical method of seeing the energy of one object moving into another object, with the key phrase being, "This ENTERS that."

Twin Aspects of Magic—purpose and method, with purpose being to draw desired energy, to repel undesired energy, or to contain desired energy while warding off undesired energy; and with method being the way the energy is manipulated through either sympathetic, comparative, directive, or transference magic, or a combination of these to achieve a desired goal.

Working Between the Worlds—moving between planes of existence, between the physical world and other worlds (astral, etheric, spiritual, etc.).

Working Name—the secret name of a Witch that is never revealed to anyone. Until a name is bestowed on the Witch by the Goddess and the God, a secret name is one created by the Witch, usually not the same as the Craft Name as this latter may be revealed to other Witches and Pagans.

Selected Bibliography

Adler, Margot. *Drawing Down the Moon; Witches, Druids, Goddess Worshippers, and Other Pagans in America Today.* Boston: Beacon Press, 1979.

Buckland, Raymond. *Buckland's Complete Book of Witchcraft.* St. Paul: Llewellyn Publications, 1994.

Cavendish, Richard. *The Black Arts.* New York: Perigee Books, The Berkley Publishing Group, 1967.

Conway, D. J. *Celtic Magic.* St. Paul: Llewellyn Publications, 1990.

Cunliffe, Barry. *The Celtic World.* New York: Greenwich House, Crown Publishers, Inc. 1986.

Cunningham, Scott. *The Complete Book of Incense, Oils, & Brews.* St. Paul: Llewellyn Publications, 1990.

Eliot, Alexander. *The Universal Myths: Heroes, Gods, Tricksters and Others.* New York: Meridian Books, 1990.

Evans-Wentz, W. Y. *The Fairy-Faith in Celtic Countries.* New York: Carol Publishing Group, 1994.

Farrar, Janet and Stewart. *A Witches' Bible: The Complete Witches' Handbook.* Custer: Phoenix Publishing, Inc., 1981.

Gimbutas, Marija. *The Civilization of the Goddess, the World of Old Europe.* Edited by Joan Marler. San Francisco: Harper-Collins Publishers, 1991.

González-Wippler, Migene. *The Complete Book of Spells, Ceremonies, Magic.* St. Paul: Llewellyn Publications, 1988.

Graves, Robert. *The White Goddess, a Historical Grammar of Poetic Myth.* New York: The Noonday Press, Farrar, Straus and Giroux, amended and enlarged edition, 1966.

Green, Marian. *A Witch Alone.* London: The Aquarian Press, 1991.

Lust, John. *The Herb Book.* New York: Bantam Books, 1974.

Mindell, Earl. *Earl Mindell's Herb Bible*. New York: Simon & Schuster, 1992.

Moura, Ann (Aoumiel). *Green Witchcraft: Folk Magic, Fairy Lore & Herb Craft*. St. Paul: Llewellyn Publications, 1996.

———. *Green Witchcraft II: Balancing Light and Shadow*. St. Paul: Llewellyn Publications, 1998.

———. *Green Witchcraft III: The Manual*. St. Paul: Llewellyn Publications, 2000.

———. *Origins of Modern Witchcraft: The Evolution of a World Religion*. St. Paul: Llewellyn Publications, 2000.

Scott, Michael. *Irish Folk & Fairytale Omnibus*. UK: Sphere Books Ltd., 1983 & 1984; New York: Barnes & Noble Books, 1983.

Squire, Charles. *Celtic Myth and Legend*. Newcastle: Newcastle Publishing Co., Inc., 1975.

Starhawk. *The Spiral Dance, A Rebirth of the Ancient Religion of the Great Goddess*. New York: HarperCollins Publishers, 1989.

Thorsson, Edred. *The Book of Ogham: The Celtic Tree Oracle*. St. Paul: Llewellyn Publications, 1992.

———. *Northern Magic: Mysteries of the Norse, Germans & English*. St. Paul: Llewellyn Publications, 1992.

Williams, Jude C. *Jude's Herbal Home Remedies*. St. Paul: Llewellyn Publications, 1996.

Index

�*) REACH FOR THE MOON

Llewellyn publishes hundreds of books on your favorite subjects! To get these exciting books, including the ones on the following pages, check your local bookstore or order them directly from Llewellyn.

Order by Phone
- Call toll-free within the U.S. and Canada, 1-877-NEW-WRLD
- In Minnesota, call (651) 291-1970
- We accept VISA, MasterCard, and American Express

Order by Mail
- Send the full price of your order (MN residents add 7% sales tax) in U.S. funds, plus postage & handling to:
  Llewellyn Worldwide
  P.O. Box 64383, Dept. 0-7387-0181-5
  St. Paul, MN 55164–0383, U.S.A.

Postage & Handling
- **Standard** (U.S., Mexico, & Canada)

If your order is:

$20.00 or under, add $5.00

$20.01–$100.00, add $6.00

Over $100, shipping is free

(Continental U.S. orders ship UPS. AK, HI, PR, & P.O. Boxes ship USPS 1st class. Mex. & Can. ship PMB.)

- **Second Day Air** (Continental U.S. only): $10.00 for one book + $1.00 per each additional book
- **Express** (AK, HI, & PR only) [Not available for P.O. Box delivery. For street address delivery only.]: $15.00 for one book + $1.00 per each additional book
- **International Surface Mail**: Add $1.00 per item
- **International Airmail**: Books—Add the retail price of each item; Non-book items—Add $5.00 per item

Please allow 4–6 weeks for delivery on all orders.
Postage and handling rates subject to change.

Discounts
We offer a 20% discount to group leaders or agents. You must order a minimum of 5 copies of the same book to get our special quantity price.

FREE CATALOG

Get a free copy of our color catalog, *New Worlds of Mind and Spirit*. Subscribe for just $10.00 in the United States and Canada ($30.00 overseas, airmail). Call 1-877-NEW-WRLD today!

Visit our web site at www.llewellyn.com for more information.

GREEN WITCHCRAFT
Folk Magic, Fairy Lore
& Herb Craft

Ann Moura (Aoumiel)

Very little has been written about traditional family practices of the Old Religion simply because such information has not been offered for popular consumption. If you have no contacts with these traditions, Green Witchcraft will meet your need for a practice based in family and natural Witchcraft traditions.

Green Witchcraft describes the worship of nature and the use of herbs that have been part of human culture from the earliest times. It relates to the Lord and Lady of Greenwood, the Primal Father and Mother, and to the Earth Spirits called Faeries.

Green Witchcraft traces the historic and folk background of this path and teaches its practical techniques. Learn the basics of Witchcraft from a third-generation, traditional family Green Witch who openly shares from her own experiences. Through a how-to format you'll learn rites of passage, activities for Sabbats and Esbats, Fairy lore, self-dedication, self-initiation, spellwork, herbcraft and divination.

This practical handbook is an invitation to explore, identify and adapt the Green elements of Witchcraft that work for you, today.

1-56718-690-4, 288 pp., 6 x 9, illus.   **$14.95**

GREEN WITCHCRAFT II
Balancing Light & Shadow

Ann Moura (Aoumiel)

The Green Witch is a natural witch, a cottage witch, and a solitary witch. This witch does not fear nature and the woods, but finds a sense of belonging and connection with the earth and the universe. Now, in this sequel to *Green Witchcraft,* hereditary witch Ann Moura dispels the common misunderstandings and prejudices against the "shadow side" of nature, the self, and the Divine. She presents a practical guide on how to access and utilize the dark powers in conjunction with the light to achieve a balanced magical practice and move towards spiritual wholeness.

Guided meditations, step-by-step rituals, and spells enable you to connect with the dark powers, invoke their energies, and achieve your goals through magical workings. Face your greatest fears so you can release them, create an elemental bottle to attract faery life, burn herbs to open your subconscious awareness, learn to use the ogham for travel to other worlds, recognize and name a familiar, and much more.

1-56718-689-0, 288 pp., 6 x 9, illus. $12.95

GREEN WITCHCRAFT III
The Manual

Ann Moura

An eight-class course of instruction for the Green Craft.

Green Witchcraft is a core practice of the traditions of earth magics, the Witchcraft of the Natural Witch, the Kitchen Witch, and the Cottage Witch. It is herbal, attuned to nature, and the foundation upon which any Craft tradition may be built. This book presents the Craft as a course of instruction, based on classes taught by the author. It utilizes *Green Witchcraft* as a textbook. Students will participate in assignments and practice activities as they learn techniques for circle casting, altars, divination, and spell working. Sample rituals and additional information is introduced to round out the student's instruction.

- Class One: Introduction to the Craft, Basic Equipment, Altars/Working Area
- Class Two: Green Rules of Conduct, Circle Casting
- Class Three: Casting a Learning Circle, Meditation, and Technique
- Class Four: Divinations—Crystal Ball Skrying, Black Mirror Gazing, Pendulum, Tea Leaves, Tarot, and Runes
- Class Five: Divination with the Celtic Ogham
- Class Six: Stones & Crystals, Elixir Preparations, Obsidian Skrying
- Class Seven: Consecration of a Statue, Divine Couples, Holy Days and Creating Your Own Calendar of Observances, Palmistry
- Class Eight: Spell Creating and Casting, Types of Magical Spells, Herb Craft, Oils, Candle Magics

1-56718-688-2, 264 pp., 6 x 9, illus. $12.95

EARTH, AIR, FIRE & WATER
More Techniques of Natural Magic

Scott Cunningham

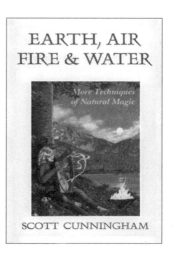

A water-smoothed stone . . . The wind . . . A candle's flame . . . A pool of water. These are the age-old tools of natural magic. Born of the Earth, possessing inner power, they await only our touch and intention to bring them to life.

The four Elements are the ancient powerhouses of magic. Using their energies, we can transform ourselves, our lives and our worlds. Tap into the marvelous powers of the natural world with these rites, spells and simple rituals that you can do easily and with a minimum of equipment. Earth, Air, Fire & Water includes more than 75 spells, rituals and ceremonies with detailed instructions for designing your own magical spells. This book instills a sense of wonder concerning our planet and our lives; and promotes a natural, positive practice that anyone can successfully perform.

0-897542-131-8, 240 pp., 6 x 9, illus.   **$9.95**

SPELL CRAFTS
Creating Magical Objects

Scott Cunningham &
David Harrington

Since early times, crafts have been intimately linked with spirituality. When a woman carefully shaped a water jar from the clay she'd gathered from a river bank, she was performing a spiritual practice. When crafts were used to create objects intended for ritual or that symbolized the Divine, the connection between the craftsperson and divinity grew more intense. Today, handcrafts can still be more than a pastime—they can be rites of power and honor; a religious ritual. After all, hands were our first magical tools.

Spell Crafts is a modern guide to creating physical objects for the attainment of specific magical goals. It is far different from magic books that explain how to use purchased magical tools. You will learn how to fashion spell brooms, weave wheat, dip candles, sculpt clay, mix herbs, bead sacred symbols and much more, for a variety of purposes. Whatever your craft, you will experience the natural process of moving energy from within yourself (or within natural objects) to create positive change.

0-87542-185-7, 224 pp., 5.25 x 8, illus., photos $10.00

THE MAGICAL HOUSEHOLD
Empower Your Home with Love, Protection, Health and Happiness

Scott Cunningham & David Harrington

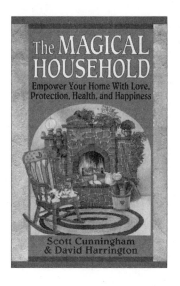

Whether your home is a small apartment or a palatial mansion, you want it to be something special. Now it can be with *The Magical Household*. Learn how to make your home more than just a place to live. Turn it into a place of security, life, fun and magic. Here you will not find the complex magic of the ceremonial magician. Rather, you will learn simple, quick and effective magical spells that use nothing more than common items in your house: furniture, windows, doors, carpet, pets, etc. You will learn to take advantage of the intrinsic power and energy that is already in your home, waiting to be tapped. You will learn to make magic a part of your life. The result is a home that is safeguarded from harm and a place which will bring you happiness, health and more.

0-87542-124-5, 208 pp., 5.25 x 8, illus. $9.95

TO STIR A MAGICK CAULDRON
A Witch's Guide to Casting and Conjuring

Silver RavenWolf

The sequel to the enormously popular *To Ride a Silver Broomstick: New Generation Witchcraft.* This upbeat and down-to-earth guide to intermediate-level witchery was written for all Witches—solitaries, eclectics, and traditionalists. In her warm, straight-from-the-hip, eminently knowledgeable manner, Silver provides explanations, techniques, exercises, anecdotes, and guidance on traditional and modern aspects of the Craft, both as a science and as a religion.

Find out why you should practice daily devotions and how to create a sacred space. Learn six ways to cast a magick circle. Explore the complete art of spell-casting. Examine the hows and whys of Craft laws, oaths, degrees, lineage, traditions, and more. Explore the ten paths of power, and harness this wisdom for your own spell-craft. This book offers you dozens of techniques—some never before published—to help you uncover the benefits of natural magick and ritual and make them work for you—without spending a dime!

Silver is a "working Witch" who has successfully used each and every technique and spell in this book. By the time you have done the exercises in each chapter, you will be well-trained in the first level of initiate studies. Test your knowledge with the Wicca 101 test provided at the back of the book and become a certified Witch! Learn to live life to its fullest through this positive spiritual path.

1-56718-424-3, 320 pp., 7 x 10, illus. **$14.95**

MAGIC FROM BRAZIL
Recipes, Spells & Rituals
Formerly released as *Saravá!*
Morwyn

Enliven your Wiccan and Magical practices with a dose of Brazilian magic

Get ready to launch yourself on an incredible journey into a fascinating cultural force and powerful magical system. Born in turn-of-the-century Brazil, the vibrant magical religions of Umbanda, Macumba, Spiritism, and Candomblé combined ecstatic African traditions with European Spiritualism. They share much in common with Wicca, shamanism, and even ceremonial magic.

This book is an insider's look at their practices, practices that you can incorporate into your own workings. Call on the powers of the Orixás, the gods of the Afro-Brazilian pantheon; practice their spellwork and rituals, trance and mediumship; experience the energies of tropical botanicals used in magic and healing; and sample Afro-Brazilian cuisine: the foods of the gods.

- This book presents authentic Brazilian magic from a Portuguese and Brazilian scholar. The author has attended ceremonies, interviewed heads of sects, recorded music, and collected artifacts for this book

- Deepens understanding of channeling, color magic, drumming, nature religions, naturopathic healing, even psychotherapy

- Introduces a refreshing perspective with important lessons for practitioners of all religions

0-7387-0044-4, 288 pp., 6 x 9, illus.   **$14.95**

ORIGINS OF MODERN WITCHCRAFT
The Evolution of a World Religion
Ann Moura (Aoumiel)

This book sheds new light on the ancient origins of religion to give Wiccans, Witches, and and Neo-Pagans a sense of where they belong in history. It is an evocative, readable account of how Pagan and mainstream beliefs evolved and interacted with each other over the centuries, written by a degreed historian. The Christian and Judaic faiths that dominate Western society and our perspectives on the nature of religion, social development, and cultural values are newcomers compared to the ancient spiritual heritage they banished through civil laws.

To assist you in searching out the historical roots of Neo-Pagan spirituality, this volume includes meditations and spells, based mainly on the major arcana of the tarot.

1-56718-648-3, 336 pp., 6 x 9, 56 illus.   **$14.95**

MAGICK FOR BEGINNERS
The Power to Change Your World

J. H. Brennan

Many magicians wear a great cloak, "the aura of dark mystery," which J. H. Brennan endeavors to remove in *Magick for Beginners*. In doing so, he introduces many aspects of magic and the occult, and explains in detail several experiments you can try for yourself, including producing a $100 bill by magic and becoming invisible.

The book is divided into two parts: Low Magick and High Magick. In Low Magick you will explore the Ouija board, astral and etheric bodies, the chakras, the aura, Qabalah, wood nymphs and leprechauns, mantra chanting, water and ghost divining, and the Tree of Life. Low Magick is fun, and serves as an introduction to the more potent system of High Magick. Here you will learn how to correctly prepare your mind before conducting ritual magic and how to conduct the rituals themselves.

1–56718–086-8, 336 pp., 5¾₆ x 8, illus.   **$9.95**